Andrew Reid

Ireland

A Book of Light on the Irish Problem

Andrew Reid

Ireland
A Book of Light on the Irish Problem

ISBN/EAN: 9783744717205

Printed in Europe, USA, Canada, Australia, Japan

Cover: Foto ©ninafisch / pixelio.de

More available books at **www.hansebooks.com**

IRELAND:

A BOOK OF LIGHT ON THE IRISH PROBLEM.

CONTRIBUTED IN UNION BY A NUMBER OF LEADING IRISHMEN AND ENGLISHMEN.

EDITED BY

ANDREW REID,
EDITOR OF "WHY I AM A LIBERAL."

LONDON:
LONGMANS, GREEN & CO.
1886.

THIS WORK

Ireland

A BOOK OF LIGHT ON THE IRISH PROBLEM

IS HUMBLY DEDICATED TO THE

Right Hon. W. E. GLADSTONE, M.P.

WITH REVERENCE AND AFFECTION

IN THE HOPE THAT AT THIS PERIOD OF

NATIONAL DARKNESS

IT MAY GIVE SOME

LIGHT

PREFACE.

IT is intended that this book shall be made a Representative Work on the Irish Problem. A number of eminent Englishmen, such as Professor FREEMAN, Sir C. GAVAN DUFFY, Professor SIGERSON, will contribute articles to a future and more complete edition of the Work, with other well-known leaders of mind in this country and the United States.

It is believed that the volume throws some strong light upon the position which the Liberal Party must occupy, and that swiftly, if it is to preserve its historical reputation, be worthy of its grand leader, and victorious in the great struggle before it. Any other position will be lower down, less secure, and less commanding. The site here indicated by wise and far-seeing men is one as lofty as it is impregnable. If you have not the courage to occupy that situation, fortified as it is by Great Principles and by Liberty herself, how can you have the courage to take up a position out in the open, which will give you no natural advantages and expose you to the withering fire of a swarm of foes?

In this work, of course, no contributor must be held answerable for the opinions of any other, though it will be seen there is complete union of sentiment among them.

PREFACE.

The article from "Leaves from a Prison Diary," by Mr. MICHAEL DAVITT—who I am sure will be of the greatest service to his country in its new era of national life—is printed here at his kind suggestion, and by the courteous permission of Mr. CHAPMAN (Messrs. Chapman, Hall & Co., Limited).

THE EDITOR.

CONTENTS.

	PAGE
INTRODUCTION	ix
ARTHUR ARNOLD	1
HON. REGINALD B. BRETT	19
MARQUIS OF LORNE	22
PROF. JAMES E. THOROLD ROGERS, M.P.	23
ALFRED RUSSEL WALLACE, LL.D.	42
ANNA BATESON	51
CHARLES BRADLAUGH, M.P.	59
REV. R. ACLAND ARMSTRONG	64
WILFRID SCAWEN BLUNT	69
A. I. TILLYARD, M.A. CAMB.	74
J. O'CONNOR POWER	77
REV. T. J. LAWRENCE	88
T. P. O'CONNOR, M.P.	96
DR. MATTHEW ROBERTSON	114
LORD MAYOR OF DUBLIN (Rt. Hon. T. D. SULLIVAN, M.P.)	121
MICHAEL DAVITT	123
A SKETCH OF IRISH HISTORY. By JUSTIN HUNTLY McCARTHY, M.P.	129
UNITED STATES CONSTITUTIONS. By OAKEY HALL	150
THE CONSTITUTION OF SWITZERLAND. By Dr. WILLIAM BURCKHARDT	156
THE DUAL SYSTEM OF GOVERNMENT OF HUNGARY AND AUSTRIA. By Dr. F. L. WEINMANN	161
STATISTICAL TABLES. Prepared by W. LEIGH BERNARD	177

INTRODUCTION.

IS the Empire in danger? What Empire? The British? There is an Empire against which, if the British people, great as they are, take up arms, they take up arms against a sea of troubles which will overwhelm them—THE EMPIRE OF LIBERTY, founded by ages of sacrifice, fortified and consolidated and made invulnerable by the blood of their fathers, the costly experience of centuries, and the long struggles of nations. This is not in danger; but the British Empire, magnificent and powerful as she is, would be, were she mad enough to wage war against it.

They laugh (you know them): "Ah, your Empire of Liberty is all sentiment; it has no army and navy, no geographical status, no money. Ah! ah! We fear it not."

Those others who have learnt the history of the world a little better than to laugh: "We do not wish to take up arms against this Empire of Liberty. We would give to Ireland the same freedom as we give to ourselves. She has the same Parliament, the same franchise as ourselves. It is not the question of liberty, but the safety of our Empire. We would not give Ireland a Parliament of her own, for it would jeopardize the Empire."

It is then a question of liberty. Your ideas of the safety of your Empire are to be the limits of the freedom of Ireland. The British Empire can only be safe by jeopardizing the liberty of Ireland, or the liberty of Ireland can only be safe by jeopardizing the security of the Empire. Is this not a profoundly melancholy situation?

Ireland can only be happy by injuring the rights of the Empire: the Empire can only be happy by injuring the rights of Ireland. What a sad and terrible strait for two nations to be in! The noble British Empire—the mother of liberty and of nations—is afraid to have near her a country possessing free institutions. Her colonies (which are thousands of leagues away) may have them. She cannot help France (who is a nearer neighbour than Ireland) having a Republic; but Ireland, the only neighbour within her power, to her she denies freedom. Is that not so?

"It is so," you say. "But it is not our fault, it is the fault of Ireland. They are a discontented people. Nothing will satisfy them."

"Nothing will satisfy them!" Why, you have just confessed that the something they want you cannot give them, and after refusing to give it you say, "Nothing will satisfy them." Either the Government makes the people, or the people makes the Government. The Government of Ireland is your Government. Are the people discontented?—you have made them discontented. Are they rebels?—you have made them rebels. Oppression manufactures rebels.

The liberty of one nation is never in conflict with the liberty of another nation. The freedom of the individual is never in conflict with the freedom of society. The rights of the one are never in hostility with the rights of the other. If so, it is not liberty; if so, they are not rights. There is a territory which belongs to the individual; there is another which belongs to society. There is one which belongs to the nation; there is another which belongs to the Empire. There is one which belongs to the Empire; there is another, wider still, which belongs to the world, to the human race, to universal society.

There is a natural and scientific frontier to each of these territories, and no individual, or people, or empire, has the right to invade them. People talk of the British Empire, but that is also subject to the universal empire of man; and both are again subject to the rights of the infant mewling and puking in the nurse's arms.

Ireland has a national territory of liberty belonging to her which is her right. It belongs to her just the same as yours belongs to you. Do you want to defend your Empire—to make her secure? You must do so within the limits of your own territory of liberty. You say: "But the interests of our Empire are greater than the interests of Ireland. Look at our vast population: the people of Ireland are nothing in comparison. Is Ireland to jeopardize the security of such a great people?"

If you wish to jeopardize your Empire—oppress. You will have a swarm of enemies. If you wish to protect the interests of your people, respect the interests and liberties of Ireland, and you will lift her up to respect the interests and liberties of England.

You say, "We are afraid of Ireland." Of course you are. You may well be afraid. Oppression will clothe the child with thunder which will shake even empires. Liberty is for the protection of the weak against the strong—of Ireland against you. It does not matter how mighty you are. Liberty is mightier, and will put into the hand of Ireland the power and opportunity which will compel you to be just.

There is no authority given by Heaven or among men which endows one nation with the permanent function to govern another. Good government always leads to liberty and free institutions. If any nation be incapable of these, the function of good government is to make them capable. The measure of the right of one community over another is the measure of capacity it is giving it, earnestly and incessantly, to rule itself. Is Ireland capable of self-government? then give it to her. Is Ireland not capable?—what more damning proof could you have that the government by England is not a good government.

I wish my countrymen to see how monstrous and dangerous it would be were we to allow the principle that the notions of safety, or even of self-preservation, which Russia or any other empire may hold, would justify her in swallowing up the liberties of other peoples. Suppose we were a small and weak nation, and France were to say, "I am afraid of England; I am a great republic; I must protect myself; I will occupy England by my army; I will smother her liberties; I will demolish her Parliament,"—would you not feel as Ireland does? And what have you to say against France or Russia, or any empire which would do such things, if you do them yourselves? I feel the shame of having to plead with my own countrymen, who are supposed to know and love liberty more than any other nation on the earth.

But an eminent judge has tried, convicted and sentenced, without jury, the whole people of Ireland to coercion, forgetting they are less criminals than ourselves :—Local institutions will lead in Ireland to a Parliament, and a Parliament will lead to the dismemberment of the Empire ; therefore, coercion.

I would sentence to penal servitude for life this learned and heartless logic :—

Coercion will lead to rebellion, rebellion will lead to revolution, revolution will lead to the dismemberment of the Empire ; therefore not coercion.

If both lead to the same goal, would it not be wiser to take the path of liberty ; and should *it* fail us, we have the consciousness within our own hearts we have trod the path of duty? If we must reap the whirlwind, let us feel we have not sown the whirlwind. Having held the scale of justice up before the eyes of the civilized world, and weighed out liberty to Ireland with no false weights—having made the scale rather dip well down on the side of Ireland—we then, if need be, can, like the Gaul, throw in the sword of the Empire, and say: "We have given you more than you ask ; the rest we must defend with our arms."

There is one thing of which I am profoundly convinced: we must not give to Ireland a mere village constitution. Even statesmen talk of " councils " and " local institutions," as if these would touch the situation. It is the national sentiment of the Irish people you have to satisfy, and you can only satisfy it, by a National Parliament. You must absorb the restless genius of the Irish people by giving them a constitution which will attract that restless genius. The first condition—which is that you must limit an Irish Parliament to the internal affairs of Ireland—imposes the second condition, that you must keep free for it as wide and important a territory of government as you can. The larger range, the more dignity, the more power you give to it, the less will she fret at those limits which you must impose upon that Parliament, and the more likely is she to have in it an assembly of calm, just, and able men, friendly to us and useful to Ireland.

ANDREW REID.

IRELAND:

A BOOK OF LIGHT ON THE IRISH PROBLEM.

ARTHUR ARNOLD.

WHY do we consider the Irish claim to be pressing, to be something to which we find no sufficient answer in the writings of the *Times*, of the Duke of Argyll, of Sir James Stephen? Why is it that we cannot say with Lord Cowper, "We need not even argue the case?" Why may we not follow that eminent jurist and judge, who can frame an indictment against a whole people in the columns of the *Times*, and so brush aside the claim for self-government with an assumption that it would be nothing but the triumph of plunder, of violence, of lawlessness? How easy, how almost enviable it seems, to be able to adopt such views! I will at once produce the key to this frame of mind and will ask if it fits the conscience of the British people. Those whom it fits will stand on one side; let those whose minds it will not unlock stand upon the other side. Is Ireland a part of the British nation? As many as are of that opinion say "Aye;" the contrary, "No." I think the Noes have it. The Noes have it. From what a mass of difficulty should we be relieved, if we, and those still more concerned, could adopt Sir James Stephen's view. It is very plain. He challenges us with this, which he dignifies by the title of "argument"—"Whatever may be really for the good of Ireland, the British Parliament can and ought to do; but it should do it itself, and on its own responsibility. A part of the nation has, or thinks it has, a grievance."

I feel bound to repudiate, as offensive to justice and to history, the doctrine that the Irish are part of the British nation. The Scotch, who by their partnership with the English have become the richest people that ever occupied so poor a country, have no cause to frown at the imputation of English nationality. But I am quite sure Mr. Goschen would never have dared to recommend his claims in Edinburgh by asserting that "after all," the Scotch are a part of the English nation. What is a nation? A body of people in number and strength sufficient to be recognised by other nations, living within well-known boundaries, and possessing sufficient communion of thought and purpose to be, as to the majority, moved by common desires natural to their condition. Ireland is a nation, so distinct that we cannot refuse to consider a claim presented by 85 to 16 of her duly elected representatives, and supported by at least 120,000 Irish voters in Great Britain, who, upon any system of proportional representation in the United Kingdom as a whole, would have been added to the electors voting in support of Irish Nationalism. Therefore I feel bound to reject Lord Cowper's view, and to consent to argue the case. If I held the view that Ireland is part of the British nation, I should imitate the brevity of Lord Cowper rather than the prolixity of Justice Stephen. There is nothing to argue if the Irish claim to self-government differs in no way from a similar claim made by the members for Kent or for Yorkshire. Then of course we should meet it with a flat negative and proceed with a perfectly free conscience to any necessary measures of coercion.

Let us be honest. Beyond all this offensive talk to Irishmen about the British nation and the British Parliament, in which their very existence is at least nominally ignored, are not we Englishmen well aware that if by four-fifths of the members for Scotland a claim like that of Ireland were presented, and a case were made out for our consideration, by which the overloaded Parliament of the United Kingdom might be relieved of all bills and questions relating to those affairs which are exclusively Scottish in their interest, we should be unanimous in denouncing any one who declared that " we need not even argue the case ?" But in the matter of Ireland, statesmen and jurists are not ashamed to assume that in the most bloodless election Ireland has probably ever seen, four-fifths of her representatives are elected to pursue a policy of plunder with the aids of outrage and assassination. A lawyer may frame, a free people cannot endorse such an accusation. Representative institutions are but a snare and a mockery, the august mother of free Parliaments is a cheat and a humbug, if, when a claim is thus presented, we are not bound by all the most sacred obligations of pride, of honour, and of duty, to argue and to examine the case.

Admitting, then, that Ireland is a nation, with powerful sentiments and even with interests which it has never been proposed to make subject to identical law, I proceed in the effort to arrive at a common understanding by putting the inquiry,—What are the limits which the conscience of the British people places upon this claim? Are there matters upon which they will cease from argument, and will apply their superior might? There may be a Scottish dukes' paradise and an English judges' paradise, in which the dwellers assume that the British people will exercise force in Ireland with denial of all discussion. That is a very dangerous dwelling. It is our most urgent duty to make plain to the Irish people those points of positive resistance. If we refuse to argue the case, and proceed, as would be necessary, to govern Ireland with as little regard to representative institutions as though she had none, then might not the question arise, whether we should not offer to foreign countries a possible case for intervention? The people's conscience would sanction—nay more, it would applaud—the armed investment of Ireland by Great Britain against any foreign invader. But if under existing circumstances we refused to argue the claim of Ireland, should we not be giving a dangerous incitement to foreign intervention? We are bound to protect ourselves against any foreign occupation of Ireland. Such a proceeding would be justifiable as a measure of self-preservation. The British have never been afraid of war. I agree entirely with Mr. Mill, that "it is not the greatest evil a nation can suffer. War is an ugly thing, but not the ugliest of things: the degraded state of moral and patriotic feeling which thinks nothing worth a war, is worse." Let it be understood, then, that we will fight for the unity of the Empire. The foreign relations of Ireland must be ours also. This is the logic of a law older and more obligatory than that of nations—the law of geographical conditions and circumstances. Lord Russell once said: "I should have been very glad if the leaders of popular opinion in Ireland had so modified and mollified their demand for Home Rule as to make it consistent with the unity of the Empire." I quote those words to show that Mr. Gladstone's limitation upon the demand for Home Rule is the same as that of his predecessor in the leadership of the Liberal party. But this is simply the refusal of absolute separation. It means that Ireland cannot be permitted to form a separate sovereignty. It matters little, but such a divorce has never to my knowledge been claimed by any responsible leader of the Irish people. Whenever this is said of Mr. Parnell, reference is always made to words he is alleged to have used somewhere in the United States, expressing his wish to destroy the "last link" of connection between Great Britain and Ireland. I think I have heard him disavow those words in the House of Commons. It is not, however, of much consequence what he meant, seeing that he has been careful not to repeat them. Obviously these words do not of necessity imply more than those he has used in Ireland, in claiming a domestic legislature, dealing with matters exclusively of Irish interest.

"The unity of the Empire, and all the authority of Parliament necessary for the conservation of that unity," are, however, quite compatible with giving to Ireland institutions such as those which obtain in self-governing colonies of the British Empire. I do not see that we are called upon to open the door to arguments quite so wide in their scope. Mr. Justin McCarthy is of all the Irish party the most highly trained in statecraft. He has nothing of the ascendancy or the dogged will of Mr. Parnell. One of the difficulties of the time lies in the fact that Mr. Parnell has never been a student of politics. In days to come he may be regarded as a sort of Irish Washington. But his contemporaries know that he is by nature somewhat of a dreamy politician, whom circumstances, including his Irish-American parentage and observation, have forced into a position which has been to no one a greater surprise than to himself. Mr. Parnell, however, has won his position by the power—which is all his own, and is a very uncommon property—of defying British opinion with a cold, silent, and most disdainful manner in the House of Commons. It was this character, never before displayed from year to year by any Irish gentleman, which gained for Mr. Parnell the confidence of the disaffected Irish. "Here is a man," they said, "who, with perfect indifference to British feeling, without brag, or blarney, or bluster, has carried obstruction to lengths which have forced recognition from Parliament." It has been as plain to them as to us who have sat with him in the House of Commons, that with Liberal and Tory Governments alike Mr. Parnell has negotiated for the introduction or the passing of Bills upon the basis of his power in reference to other legislation. He is now possessed of an authority by which he can nullify at his pleasure the most useful and effective of the Rules of 1882. By securing the attendance of forty of his band he can on any and every night compel the Speaker to choose between remaining in the chair to hear Irish members discuss some "definite matter of urgent public importance," or applying the *clôture*, with perhaps doubtful authority. Whatever else may happen, it is not unlikely to be quickly demonstrated that the new Rules are inadequate to the needs of Parliament. For such work Mr. Parnell's methods are invaluable. He is not equally qualified to discuss the details of a political settlement. At all events, Mr. Justin McCarthy has perceived that it is useless to ask in the case of Ireland for the legislative powers of a self-governing colony, because Ireland is too near to Great Britain and too remote from any foreign country to render it possible for the larger island to admit of conditions in Ireland which might tend towards separation. We desire with ever-increasing ardour the maintenance of imperial union with the Colonies, but we should not fight for that matter against the persistent will of four-fifths of the members of the Colonial Legislatures. If Canada should desire to be merged with the United States, she is free to form a continental union. If Australia should wish to become the seat of a solitary empire or of a great republic, she too is free to follow an independent existence apart from that of the mother-country. But Ireland can never in this sense be independent. Just as New Guinea is bound by physical laws stronger than those of humanity to Australia, and will never act in total separation from the larger island; just as Sicily is bound to Italy; so is Ireland bound to Great Britain. Therefore we may, with Mr. Justin McCarthy, draw the words of limitation closer than those of Lord Russell and Mr. Gladstone, and may proclaim the unity of the kingdom to be the indissoluble, the ineffaceable basis of all argument. We cannot recognise any menace to the title and sovereign authority of the United Kingdom, which are as dear to us, are as certainly objects for which any conceivable sacrifices of life and treasure would be made with heroism, with devotion, with success, as were such title and authority in the case of the people of the United States. I am quite prepared to admit the possibility that the United Kingdom of Great Britain and Ireland may become more truly united by a change of the constitution such as shall bring it into greater resemblance to that of the United States of America.

Then it is said: "Are you afraid of 86 members in a Parliament of 670? Is it possible you can admit this matter to argument, because you think to get rid of obstruction in the House of Commons? Are not the 584 able to secure the proper progress of business and that due respect for the will of the majority to which you seem disposed to pay attention in Ireland?" I own I am much surprised at this line of argument. Of course, Mr. Parnell and his band, together with 3,000,000 of unarmed, unorganized Irish people, are impotent against the legislative and military might of Great Britain. If the dynamite faction, which has been, I suspect, a much greater terror to Mr. Parnell than to the British public, were multiplied by hundreds, we should listen less to the claims of Ireland while we perfected a system for trapping and destroying these inhuman beasts of prey. No, we are not fearful of anything but to do wrong. We are afraid of being unjust. We can fight with the terrible resistless warfare of Ironsides; but our conscience must go, clean and wholly, with us into civil battle. There are certain things we cannot do. We cannot give a full and free suffrage to Ireland in 1884, and then assert in 1886 that the overwhelming verdict of the Irish people is of no consequence. We cannot uphold representative institutions and stifle the voice of four-fifths of the representatives of one of the three nations. We must listen to their claim as to one presented with an extraordinary and commanding body of assent. We cannot but frown shame on those who, without ears to hear, try to persuade us that this determination of the great majority of the Irish nation is nothing but an enterprise of plunder and lawlessness. It does not follow that we must admit their claim; but we are bound in honour and duty to examine it with the deepest interest, attention, and respect. We hold that to refuse to argue such a case may be to incur the guilt of an incitement and an encouragement to lawlessness and crime.

Now, what is the case? Mr. Mill said: "Before admitting the authority of any persons, as organs of the will of the people, to dispose of the whole political existence of a country, I ask to see whether their credentials are from the whole or only from a part." First, then, we have, including, as we are bound, the unopposed elections, the verdict of a clear majority of the electors of Ireland. We have the evidence of 85 to 16 elected members. We have the complaint of the minority in nearly all parts of the country of the overwhelming influence of the Nationalist party. The loud claim of the minority forms an extremely important element in our rejection of any scheme of separation. The demand for home government is not universal, though it is immensely preponderant. We have in these circumstances to consider what is our duty, what is the interest of the Irish people and our own interest, in the matter? All are agreed that we must for common purposes maintain unity in the supreme government of the United Kingdom. We should no doubt obtain from Irish members valuable aid in reducing the cost of imperial government.

The Crown lands in Ireland are not worth more than £300 a year; from quit-rents reserved in ancient grants the Crown is entitled to receive about £40,000 a year from Ireland; and that is the whole of the Crown property in Ireland. I repudiate as absurd, for Irishmen as for Englishmen, the suggestion that they should make any payment to imperial revenues without representation in the Imperial Parliament. The days of taxation without representation are past and gone. The public debt is undoubtedly that of the United Kingdom. One of the first questions to be considered would be the nature, amount, and the consequences of the contribution from Ireland to imperial expenditure.

In consenting to argue the case, we assume that an agreement has been established to do so without reference to separation. We take for our basis the plan of the United States, which is not a federation of States, but of peoples. We preserve the Union. We admit no right in separate legislatures to infringe the Union. In the United States there is no federation of legislatures or of territories. When a common act is done, the proclamation does not run "We, the States, proclaim," or "The Legislatures of the States proclaim;" it runs, in all common concerns, "We, the people of the United States." The possible modification we are considering of the constitution of the United

Kingdom would, we may suppose, be quite external to all those matters which are in the United States within the domain of Congress. Throughout the Union, Congress has power to levy and collect taxes, duties, imposts, and excises, to pay the debts, to provide for the common defence and general welfare, to borrow money, to regulate commerce, to establish uniform naturalisation and bankruptcy laws, to coin money, to fix the standards of weights and measures and punish counterfeiting, to establish post offices and postal lines, to register patents and copyrights, to punish piracies, to declare war, raise armies and navies, to call out the militia, and to govern all places purchased for forts and arsenals. The several States of the Union possess all powers of local legislation, but they cannot make treaties, coin money, levy duties on imports, or exercise without consent any of the powers thus granted to Congress. The Supreme Court of the United States has jealously guarded the legal rights of Congress. When a State entered into a contract with certain Indians to except their lands from taxation, it was held that the exemption could not be revoked. The most learned writers on the American constitution have shown that the idea of a permanent and zealous co-operation of the several distinct governments in any scheme for the common welfare is a visionary notion. They have shown that the navigation and commerce, the agriculture and manufactures of all the States have received an advancement in every direction throughout the Union which has far exceeded the most sanguine expectations of the warmest friends of the constitution, and they have described the fact of an unlimited commercial intercourse, without duty or restriction, between all the States, as of itself a blessing of almost inconceivable value. There was a time in the independent history of Ireland when her people were taxed £350,000 a year to prevent the importation of British cottons. Following the pattern of the United States, there could be no revival of such injurious laws. The customs and excise system would remain one in all the United Kingdom.

It is not difficult to disentangle the "loyalty" of certain classes in Ireland from their interest as landowners. The distinction must be drawn. They are loyal, but we should hear less of their loyalty if they could sell their Irish land at a good figure. I am not disposed to think their interests would suffer by such a change as we are considering. No law of an Irish Parliament could upon this basis annul the contract to pay judicial rent, nor transfer ecclesiastical possessions from the Protestant Episcopal to the Roman Catholic Church. No State Legislature in America has any power to destroy contracts. The Irish landlords and others of the Irish minority have strong claims, but they cannot demand that we should accept no change without being prepared to purchase their interest in their country.

It is no answer to considerations such as these to suggest that stipulations of this sort, even if agreed to at the time of an amendment of the constitution, would not be observed by the Irish people. Our effort is not only to soothe Irish disaffection by every useful and proper means, but also to reach firm ground, on which, if need be, we can with a free conscience compel the obedience of Ireland. There are millions of English people, and their number is increasing every day, who cannot consent to make war upon Ireland, without an offer of the grant of some such institutions. I have been many times in Ireland, but never without a distinct feeling that she needs a measure of Home Rule; that it would be good for all; that a country so large and so distinct, but without any local legislative power, is in an unwholesome unnatural condition.

We may now progress in the supposition that, under these and possibly other limitations, a legislature may be granted to Ireland. Whether there should be one or two Chambers would be fair matter for argument. I think the Senate of the United States is chargeable with the inferior character of the House of Representatives; that it lowers the tone of the first Chamber by abstraction of the best men, and by making it less responsible. I should prefer a single Chamber, and we may suppose that there would be one such legislative body in each of the three kingdoms. This would of course involve the eligibility of peers. The numbers might respectively be those of each kingdom in the Imperial Parliament, or larger if that were desirable. There need be no identity in the *personnel* of the local legislature and of the contingent to the Imperial Parliament. A great Liberal statesman of the last generation had a plan for establishing three such local Parliaments in Ireland: one for Munster and Connaught, one for Ulster, and another for Leinster. Of course, if Ireland preferred two legislatures, one for Northern and another for Southern Ireland, so much the better; but it is of no use to set up such division against the wishes of the people. I cannot conceive that such a legislature would, under the limitations we have noted, be more unfavourable to the interests of property than the present condition. The apprehension of a strike against rent has been no novelty for many years. The fear of such a movement has found expression in the speeches of statesmen throughout the century. I am quite disposed to think that Irish landlords would find in such a change better security for their property than in dragoons and armed policemen. The perpetual employment of armed force is impossible, and every application of it, without promise of home government, diminishes the value of the landlords' claim. Their hope is to get out of Ireland by some measure at the cost of the general treasury. But Parliament has made its farthest possible advance in that direction. I declare most sincerely, that if I were an Irish landlord and regarded nothing but my own interests, I would rather rest my hopes upon a resolute and combined appeal in an Irish Legislature than endure the wasting process which is now in prospect.

The Government and people of Ireland may still be described in the words of Grattan : " A people ill-governed, and a Government ill-obeyed." One of the standing grievances of the Irish people is, that they contribute too much to the general revenue. I think the basis of their payment was unjustly fixed at the time of the Union. Mr. Jephson, in a very clever publication on the financial aspect of Home Rule, adds together the common charges for national debt, civil list, army and navy, legislature, foreign and colonial service, and for civil functionaries, makes the total in round numbers £60,000,000, and proceeds, upon the Union basis, to divide this total into "15 parts for Great Britain and 2 for Ireland," making Ireland's contribution a little over £7,000,000. It is suggested that this question of contribution would be a subject for endless difference. I think it would be so if the rude principles of the Union were continued. How did Lord Castlereagh arrive at the conclusion that the proportion was 15 to 2, or roughly 7 to 1? Ireland had then a totally separate system of customs and excise. There was no assessment for property and income tax. He had regard to the exports and imports of the two islands, and to the consumption of various commodities. He found that for 1798 the total trade of Ireland was £10,925,916; that of Great Britain, £73,961,299. He observed that in the consumption of seven commodities most in demand, the proportion was $7\frac{7}{8}$ to 1. Upon these and similar facts the contribution was fixed at 15 parts for Great Britain and 2 for Ireland; an arrangement which, as Mr. Jephson says, lasted until the amalgamation of exchequers and of debts in 1816. It will be remembered that the relative proportion of the populations was at that time very different. The data of 1798 are no longer available, for no one can now distinguish with certainty the amount of customs or excise paid by Ireland. Of 1,000 chests of tea which pay duty in Liverpool, any number may be sent across to Ireland, where no duty would be payable. But we have far more accurate data than those which were at the command of Lord Castlereagh.

We have the figures of income tax. In Ireland, the system of assessment and collection is different from that in force in England and Scotland; but the difference is rather in the official machinery than in the result, which is the fairest test of the ability of the two islands in regard to contribution. By the Act of Union, Great Britain and Ireland "united as to future expenses on a strict measure of relative ability." Those who adopt the measure of 15 to 2 at the present time could not be regarded as strict in adherence to truth or justice. The income tax returns for the year 1882-83 are conclusive. Schedules A, B, and D for Great Britain give a total of £446,629,197; for Ireland, £33,269,668; a proportion of nearly 13½ to 1.

In most calculations the Civil List and the National Debt are charged just as they stand in the estimates, to be paid in part by Ireland. But the Civil List charge is satisfied by the income of the Crown Lands Department. Irishmen may claim to examine the settlement of the Debt in 1800-16. The annual charge in 1799 for the debt of Great Britain was £18,000,000, and of the Irish debt about £1,400,000. There can be no doubt that the debt of Great Britain was due in part to the cost of protecting Ireland equally with the shores of this island. I think the charge for imperial concerns admits of reduction; there are many sinecures to be weeded out, many salaries are much too high, and the age of compulsory superannuation is certainly too low. Taking it at the present average of

£55,000,000, the contribution of Ireland upon the basis of the income tax would be about £4,000,000.

But it may be said: "Where is the use of discussing this proportion when the real question is, How will you make Ireland pay? Take Limerick for example, and the present refusal to defray the charge for police. It seems to me that the case of Limerick does not at all weaken the force of the arguments of the Irish majority; rather the contrary. We hesitate as to Limerick, because we know Ireland is ill-governed, and because we are sure that on the whole the game would not be worth the candle. But in that of the imperial contribution we cannot fail to admit that no just man would hesitate to take action. The imperial force would, if necessary, levy the charge, supported by the whole strength of British opinion and of whatever was just in Irish opinion. No difficulty is found in the United States in executing the decrees of the Supreme Court. Such a failure as that at Limerick could never occur.

The veto is a most important point. It does not appear to me that the veto could or need be placed directly within the power of the Imperial Parliament. A Bill passed by the States of Jersey is not law until sanctioned by the Queen in Council, and by custom the Council advising Her Majesty is formed exclusively of Ministers of the Crown. Parliament has therefore indirect control over the legislation of Jersey by withdrawing its confidence from the Government. But this power would be inconsistent with a change such as would devolve certain affairs upon local Legislatures in Great Britain and in Ireland, or in each of the three kingdoms. If the change were made only in respect to Ireland, it would soon follow in regard to Scotland. In the United States the veto of the President and the power of Congress do not extend to Bills dealing with matters within the restricted domain of the State Legislatures. But in fact the veto would be with the Imperial Government, because the Crown would nominate the viceroy or governor of Ireland. If he were subject to removal by the Crown, as are the governors of our colonies, the power of vetoing any Bill would be that of the Crown, which, if not advised in these matters by Imperial Ministers, would not be free from their influence.

It is no lightsome duty to contemplate a great change in our constitution. We altered the balance of power in 1867 and in 1884, but the writing of certain provisions into our constitution, involving changes of legislative authority, is a different matter. We must not do it in haste or without due cause. I have not dealt largely with the cause. Some will think the recent annals of Parliament are eloquent upon that point. Others feel that any concession is matter of justice or of expediency which would liberate their consciences and enable them, if need be, to draw the sword of justice against Ireland. I have rather chosen to assume that the motives for consideration of the claim are admitted. If there were no good reason, even the strongest would shrink from the task. Boldness is, according to Lord Bacon, the first quality of a statesman; and it will be needed. "You might as well ask me to build a tree," said Lord Holland to Murat when the new King of Naples asked for the draught of a constitution. But we must remember that this claim of Ireland occurs at a time when Parliament has been found incompetent for the legislative work of the Empire. What precious years have we not wasted through this century in the effort to bind a Protestant system of education upon Ireland! How natural it seemed to us, when the Australian Colonies desired a Federal Council Bill, to tell them to wait a year! That is nothing in our legislative economy. We want and wait through one or two generations. So it has been with Land Law Reform; so it may be with Church Reform. This Irish demand is entertained the more readily because it may summon us to a wise, just, and beneficial revolution, valuable not only to each of the three kingdoms, but to every portion of the Empire. For many years past there have been warnings of coming change. The late Lord Russell was no Radical, and his most mature thought found the following expression :—

"I do not think the relations of the colonies to the mother country can be kept up precisely in their present form. I am disposed to believe that if a congress or assembly, representing Great Britain and her dependencies, could be convoked from time to time, to sit for some months in the autumn, arrangements reciprocally beneficial might be made. The scheme may seem impracticable to many. But so did the Reform Act of 1832; so did the total repeal of the Corn Laws; so did the abolition of the Irish Church. Great changes have been made; great changes are impending; amid these changes there is no greater benefit to mankind that a statesman can propose to himself than the consolidation of the British Empire."

The time may soon come when the peoples of England, Ireland, and Scotland may be represented only in regard to common affairs by a Parliament of the United Kingdom, which may also be a Congress of the Empire. We may in days to come regard this pressure from Ireland even with grateful recollection, as having supplied the motive power for a useful reform. It may happen that in this Parliament of the future the federalisation of the Australian continent, or the reform of the Government of India, may be deemed of equal, if not greater and more pressing consequence, than the place of a blow-hole on the Underground Railway, or than a debate such as that of 1885, as to whether an Edinburgh hotel-keeper should or should not have to face the competition of another hotel at a railway station. No one will say that our Parliamentary system is perfect; it attempts too much; and the most contentious business, which is the most important, is consequently postponed from year to year. If we are to have change, let it be large as the principle involved, so that it may be lasting, and let us in all its provisions be careful to preserve that which has been held sacred by Liberal leaders since the dawn of reform—" the unity of the Empire, and all the authority of Parliament necessary for the conservation of that unity."

ARTHUR ARNOLD.

HON. REGINALD B. BRETT.

IS it not a fact, that for more than a century we have attempted to govern Ireland constitutionally?

Has the experiment succeeded?

Is it not probable that the failure is due largely to differences of race and religion?

. What analogous cases are there in history?

Are not Austria-Hungary, Russia-Poland, the least dissimilar?

What were the methods respectively adopted in these cases?

Is not the successful stamping-out of rebellion and national life in Poland due to the circumstance that Russia was able to employ the coercive forces of a despotic form of government?

Did not the liberation of Hungary result from the circumstance that Austria was only able to apply constitutional methods in the government of Hungary, and that the inevitable result is the Autonomy of that nation?

Is not the case of the rebellion in the United States wholly different, because no ineradicable difference of race or creed divided North from South?

Is there any responsible statesman who now proposes to govern Ireland permanently by Martial Law?

Is there any large section of politicians who would advocate permanent application to Ireland of coercive measures?

Does the experience of the past afford much hope that party spirit will allow of a permanent combination of

Liberals and Conservatives in the House of Commons against the Irish Representatives?

There cannot be any serious difference of opinion upon the answer to these questions; but it is when we come to the inference to be drawn from them that the inclination to shrink from logical conclusions appears. Surely the experience of the past teaches us that timidity is the essence of Conservatism, and that no great reform has ever been carried through Parliament without honest prognostications, founded on the most honest conviction, that the country was going inevitably to the devil.

Men who maintain that the Irish people cannot be trusted in any degree because some Irishmen have behaved brutally and dishonestly, ought to recollect that in 1832 it was stated often, and believed, that the English people could not be trusted because some Englishmen had behaved riotously and illegally. Austrians, before Count Beust carried his constitutional reforms, never wearied of pointing out that concessions to Hungarian sentiment meant the destruction of the Empire.

Because Catholics supported the Pretender, how long was it before the majority of Englishmen could be got to believe that their Catholic fellow-countrymen could be patriots?

And after Lord Somers' Scottish Union, when Lord Chatham, with the brilliant audacity of genius, enrolled Highland regiments in the service of the State, how often was he told that he was drilling men whose arms would on the first opportunity be turned against their commanders?

Now, in another form, the old story is repeated. From the editors of the great metropolitan daily papers down to their eminent judicial correspondents, there is a chorus of doubt and distrust. No Sovereign Parliament for the United Kingdom could control a National Council for

Ireland. That is the burden of their cry. The facts that in Germany a Sovereign Parliament controls Local Legislatures, that in America the same thing occurs, that in the British Empire the most complete control is exercised by the Imperial Parliament over the Colonial Legislatures—these facts do not convince them, or even shake their belief, that they may misjudge the Irish problem.

Some time ago, before the startling so-called revelations from Hawarden appeared, I suggested the appointment of a Committee or Commission, representative of the two great parties in the State, and of the Irish party as well, to inquire into the present system of Irish administration, which is not understood by the majority of Englishmen, with a view to determining the limits within which Irish affairs can be administered locally, and the form of local government best suited to the requirements and resources of that country, consistent with the sovereignty of the Imperial Parliament.

I still think such an inquiry desirable, and the course most likely to lead to practical results.

Professor Seeley says, in his "History of Napoleon," that to be simply an emperor, to rule a country through an army, is to practise an easy art. It may be that we shall have to practise the easy art of governing Ireland by the sword. But who can doubt that this as a permanent policy will not meet the views of the English people? Consequently, statesmen will have sooner or later to grapple with the more difficult problem.

If civil war is inevitable, it will cause less bitterness and lead to a surer peace after the experiment of Home Rule has failed than before it has been tried.

REGINALD B. BRETT.

MARQUIS OF LORNE.

IRELAND depends financially on British connection. Geographically she must remain an integral part of the Imperial Three Kingdoms. Anything tending to throw her into antagonism to England and Scotland would harm her by driving away capital. Therefore, all armed forces and all departments expressive of sovereignty must be Imperial. Property acquired under Imperial title cannot be expropriated. Home Rule, if it mean power to acquire property by purchase, and the subsequent control over it by provincial bodies, may work for good. Assessory powers might be given to provincial areas for education and repayment of Imperial loans for purchase of property. County Councils might have similar powers for purposes requiring less money. The same purpose of multiplying freeholds and endowing education could be attained by constitution of separate Boards acting for the whole country. The powers asked for by the so-called National Party would be given by no American or colonial statesmen, whose chief care has been to prevent any unit of population from acquiring power which might be used to the disadvantage of the nation.

LORNE.

PROF. JAMES E. THOROLD ROGERS, M.P.

MEMBERS of Parliament who may take office, members of Parliament who are in office, and the Tory party generally, who profited by the Irish alliance at the late General Election, and who now appear to be repudiating their allies, are equally shy of stating what opinions they hold on the Irish question. From the point of view of party tactics it is not reasonable that statesmen out of office, but in waiting, should be called on to break silence. Nor is it strange, or even indecent, that the Government of Caretakers should be hesitating. It is a tradition with the Tory party to make very few promises, and the practice with them to break the few they do make. They never can and never will satisfy their followers and dupes. It would be instructive to illustrate the facts, but it would be a lengthy labour, and in the present case irrelevant. There is, however, no reason why men who do not expect office, who have given attention to public affairs, and are responsible to their constituents, should affect to be silent or oracular in the present crisis. It is the duty of such persons, however humble their political status may be, especially in face of the fact that more than half the present House of Commons are new men, not to affect silence, however abstinent they may have been in expressing their opinion when they were before their constituents.

Let me briefly narrate the political history of Ireland. When its Parliament of English settlers was first established, it was, as all the world knows, regulated by Poyning's Act, the one feature of which was that no legislative topic could be debated, and no Bill introduced into the Irish Parliament, but by the express permission of the English Government. This was no particular servitude under the Tudors, for the English Parliament had not much greater initiatory power ; and the Scottish Parliament was, as Scotch constitutional antiquaries know, equally subjected to the Lords of the Articles. But the English Parliament emancipated itself, by the use of very energetic remedies, from the Crown, only to fall for nearly two centuries under the control of the House of Lords. The Scotch Parliament was incorporated about one hundred and eighty years ago with the English Parliament, and the Scotch nobility—the most turbulent, corrupt, sordid, and rapacious aristocracy which has ever been heard or read of—was fortunately attenuated in the English House of Lords. But the Irish Parliament remained in the chains of Poyning's Act for nearly three centuries. It represented about a fourth of the people, but of the Protestants only, or rather such of those persons as were qualified to vote. All the members had to belong to the dominant religion of the minority, and so absolutely dead was political feeling in Ireland that there was no real movement in the country, even when the most stirring passions were dominant in England and elsewhere.

At last the awakening came. The foolish and wicked war with the American colonies brought England apparently more near prostration than at any time in her political or military history. It was really the King's war, and should be a caution for the English people never to let their sovereigns meddle in foreign politics. The sequel to it shows that the sovereign should be equally debarred from meddling in domestic politics, for the folly of George the Third was the beginning of the Irish difficulty.

In 1779 the Irish were admitted by North to the benefits

of the English trade. In 1782 the Irish were, under the narrow franchise and sectarian conditions alluded to above, indulged by Fox with a replica of the English constitution. They were allowed to levy their own taxes, administer their own affairs, regulate their own trade, appoint their own officials, manage their own army, and decide their own appeals in their own House of Lords, as Englishmen were in theirs. The surrender was complete—a surrender which Irishmen in our own day, and indeed for the last fifty years and more, have looked back to as the great charter of Irish liberty. If any one wishes to know how Irishmen thought and spoke when they gained the freedom of initiation as well as debate —even though, I repeat, the speakers were the representatives of a narrow section out of a narrow Irish majority—let him read the debate on Orde's Bill for regulating British and Irish commerce, in May 1785.

The history of these memorable eighteen years has never been written, and yet these years are the cradle of Irish political opinion in the eighteenth century, and the key to Irish political opinion in the nineteenth. The Government which granted the constitution of 1782 began to conspire against it immediately. They had taken Poyning's Act away from the beginning of its proceedings, and they clapped it on to the end of its proceedings, as effectually as if the change had not been made. They developed in the Irish mind that distrust of all government which has made it so turbulent and so docile—turbulent to its administrators, docile to its popular leaders. To reward an Irishman with office was to make him hateful to his countrymen; and to be just, the most merciless oppressors of Irishmen were Irishmen. I do not think that politics ever bred a worse man than Lord Clare, and I am equally convinced that law has rarely produced a harder and more cruel one. The Irish showed what they thought of the man at his funeral.

The insurrection of 1797–8 was the end of the free Irish

Parliament. English statesmen had before them these alternatives: They might yield to the claims of the United Irishmen, emancipate the Catholics, and trust to the effects of justice and political responsibility. This was what Pitt and Fitzwilliam wished, but the King strongly forbade it. There was the alternative of ruling Ireland as a Crown colony, without a constitution, and by a Privy Council of nominees. This was forbidden by English public opinion, by the state of public affairs, by the experience of the United States, and by the military dangers which beset the situation. The third alternative was the Parliamentary Union. To effect this it was necessary to corrupt the borough-mongers, and, as Irishmen tell us, the Union was purchased from the Irish aristocracy by hard British cash. The Irish Parliament was closed, and its premises let to a bank, where I presume the vendors invested the price which they had received.

From 1800 begins a double struggle in Ireland: a struggle for the equitable occupation of land, and a struggle for the restoration of that Parliament which, as time passed, the fond memory of the Irish has decorated with every virtue. The administrations of Ireland had one expedient for disaffection, and that was a special criminal code for the island. The late Sir Robert Peel said, with excusable exaggeration, that he had never gone through a session in his parliamentary career without taking part in a Scotch Salmon Bill and an Irish Coercion Bill. But to every claim of tenant right, to every demand that the religious sentiments of the Irish should be respected and deferred to, the English Parliament was obstinately deaf. Even toleration, the most hateful word in politics, was refused for some thirty years after the Union. Nearly three-quarters of a century passed before the dominant Church of the minority was reconstructed; more than this period passed before a system of equitable rents was made a principle in the social politics of Ireland. Meanwhile, as may be expected, when justice is tardy, discontent becomes envenomed, and the Irish, in a fit of petulance, which they call principle, have preferred their worst foes in a general election, to their cautious, lukewarm, but, for all that, historic friends.

The revolt of the Irish—a parliamentary revolt it is true, for none of them, except a few hair-brained fanatics, think of force—is complete. No manipulation of figures can dispute that Mr. Parnell's followers represent current Irish opinion. I decline to believe that a nation terrorizes itself, or that the stupendous majorities by which the eighty-five were returned are an illustration of successful tyranny imposed by an ubiquitous organization. The representatives of ancient Whiggery, of modern Orangeism, of more modern Toryism, in contrast to which I admit the Toryism of England is gentle and generous, are cooped up in the north east corner of the island, in which they talk as Walker did not when the Anglo-Irish had experience of Tyrconnel's Parliament, and of the rapparees, whose name they have adopted. Once, by an accident no doubt, though he may have been misreported, that Parliament was declared by Mr. Parnell to be his ideal. The history of it, perhaps heightened, may be found in Macaulay's twelfth chapter.

I think it may be taken for granted that special criminal legislation for Ireland—the tradition of the English Government since the Union, the practice of the Government for centuries before it—will not be revived. I am pretty confident that if the late Government had proceeded with the proposal which was foreshadowed before the defeat on the Budget, the Liberals below the gangway would have deserted them. I have little doubt that this was the reason why the late Government did not attempt to reverse the very retrievable disaster of June 8. I made no secret of my resolve never to vote for another Irish Coercion Bill, and I know that my views were generally held by the advanced section of the Liberal party. It is, I think, a fundamental principle in the policy of the political unit, that its civil and criminal law should be identical in any one of the contingents which make up the unit. This has been the tradition of British law. Fifty years ago there were agrarian disturbances in England, marked by outrages as bitter and as malignant as anything which has occurred in Ireland. They were not met by local Coercion Acts, but by remedial measures. At present the Tory party is committed against coercion, and the Radical party too.

Very possibly, Lord Cowper may be in the right when he alleges that the strength of Mr. Parnell's party lies in the purposes of the Irish cottiers. I said so myself nearly eighteen years ago, when I studied the Irish land question on the spot, and wrote my conclusions in a letter to Sir John Gray, a letter which I reprinted and circulated in the House of Commons at the beginning of the late Parliament. I think it very likely that the Irish peasant farmer wants to get his rent at the lowest rate possible, and perhaps, as an Irishman (and a patriot) told me the other day, when this is achieved, to get his neighbour's farm as soon as possible. An Irishman believes, and with good reason, that he has given his land all the value it has. He does not realize the Ricardian theory of rent. He thinks maybe that he owes to the Land League the Act of 1881, and the interpretation he puts on it. Do not his newspapers say so, and does he not believe the modern sophist as fervently as the average Englishman is reputed to swallow his *Times* ?

This is not the sole motive of the revolt, though a powerful one. I wonder whether easy-going people see that the same process is going on in Great Britain. What else is the meaning of the crofter successes in North Scotland, the political discontent already almost organized in Wales, the revolt of the peasantry in the extremities of England, and the desperate efforts of imperilled landowners to hold their own by intimidation, by the passionate adoption of the Duke of Westminster's manifesto, by the "profligate lying of virtuous women," by the intimate association of parsons, publicans, primroses, and peers? But, on the other hand, if the demands of the Irish are so hateful to England, how is it that the Irish in England live so amicably with their English fellow-workmen? The alliance of the Tories and Irish in the boroughs of Lancashire and some Yorkshire towns has not stirred the English patriot in those districts to avenge himself on this portentous combination. In South and East London there is a very large Irish element: it did not raise the percentage of voters over its normal 70 to 75 per cent. of the register. In point of fact, I suspect that the English workman believes that both the historical parties are equally insincere; the Irishman, more impulsive, fancies they are equally squeezable.

An Irishman—you can see it all through the report of Sir Eardley Wilmot's Committee—is entirely convinced of the backwardness, the poverty, the hopelessness of his country. His economical remedies—for instance, those of Mr. Parkinson—may be immeasurably grotesque, but they are none the less instructive. They are the natural commentary on the process by which Ireland has been governed by Englishmen, with the best intentions, but on old Whig principles and by old Whig methods. For eighty-five years there have been tardy concessions, capricious grants of public money, and ready coercion. It may be true that the Government has been forced to employ English, because no Irishman would have had the courage, by taking office in the

Irish administration, to incur the hatred and the execrations of his fellow-countrymen. It may be doubted if in the last Parliament the office most unwisely given to Mr. Forster had been given to the O'Conor Don, or to some other Irish gentleman of such high merit and unimpeachable character, the disasters of Mr. Gladstone's Irish administration would, as I believe, have been obviated. But if it be true that an Irishman holding confidential relations with the English Government cannot retain the simultaneous confidence of his own countrymen, what a satire is the fact on the policy of the last eighty-five years! Has it come to this? Has the English Government so demoralized the Irish that they will have no confidence or trust in any Irishman who allies with it, or even negotiates with it?

Of course, as a matter of fact, Ireland, with the semblance of parliamentary equality, with the reality of parliamentary institutions, and with a slowly but fully developed power of entangling English public business, has been ruled as a Crown colony, because she has not been ruled by her own people. The highest office in the country is bestowed on an English nobleman, generally in difficulties. The Irish Secretary is the head of every department. He is Secretary of State, President of the Local Government Board, of the Board of Trade, of the Board of Works, of Education—of everything. He is now never an Irishman, he his rarely in the Cabinet, and generally his initial qualification is a profound ignorance of Ireland and Irish affairs. I confess, if I were an Irishman, and had such experiences as Irishmen have of the administration of Irish affairs, I should be tempted to be a rebel, and I should not be surprised if I were called a village ruffian.

I cannot, therefore, accept Lord Cowper's explanation of Irish disaffection as complete. That Mr. Parnell would have had but a limited success if he had relied on the

Home Rule feeling only, I can well believe. The sympathy with political reform is partial at most times. It rises to an almost revolutionary force when it is believed to be the only remedy for intolerable social evils. The enthusiasm of the *tiers état* in 1789, the uprising of the English people in 1832, were in the highest degree exceptional. But if a politician can enforce on his disciples that the only remedy for social mischief and economical degradation is a vast political change, and he can win a little of his programme from those who dread the change, he has the key of the situation in his hand. The Home Rule movement would, I daresay, have languished even if the Irish had been fed to repletion with calumnies against the English people. But the Home Rule movement, as a means for enforcing terms from the Irish landlord, has been an irresistible bait. My wonder is, that no Irish politician had previously to Mr. Parnell combined the tactics of Mr. O'Connell and those of Mr. Sharman Crawford.

The common criticism on the Irish people is, that they cannot govern their own country. If this were true, what is the good of mocking them with the semblance of parliamentary power? The true theory of the constitution is that the Ministry are the servants of the House of Commons —*i.e.*, of the English people through their representatives. A decorous fiction calls them the Ministers of the Crown, but unless we are to have the scenes of the Short and Long Parliament of 1640 re-enacted, the House of Commons makes them and unmakes them. But no one doubts that in the Scottish kingdom Scotch public opinion must be consulted. Parliament has lately created a Scotch Minister of State. The office is filled by a nobleman, a great Scottish landowner, who if he is descended from Louisa of Portsmouth, is also descended from the Duke of Gordon. Would the Scotch have been satisfied if an Englishman, without a drop of Scotch blood or a scintilla of Scotch interest, had stepped into the place? But what Irish interests do Lords Cowper, Spencer, Carnarvon, Mr. Forster, Mr. Trevelyan, and Sir W. Hart Dyke represent, excellent men as they may be, except the convenience of ulcerating Irish disaffection.

I set very little in the present situation by the weakness of Irish industry, the want of economical versatility in the Irish people, and the incessant mendicancy of Irish patriots. The Irish have been denied the responsibilities of government till they charge Government with all their misfortunes, and even refuse to give any but the vaguest answer to the natural question, What is your remedy for your own discontent? I know nothing in history like the condition of the Irish people, except that of the Spanish settlements in the New World. It is well known that there the Spanish Government not only administered colonial affairs from Madrid, but debarred even the purest-blooded Spaniard who was born in the colony from filling any responsible office in it. Every one who was to be trusted with public business was sent from Spain. Can it be a pride to the English race that it has by hard pains and little wisdom, in aristocratic interests, bred a Mexico or a Peru at its very doors, which it cannot trust with its own affairs, from which it receives year after year intolerable affronts, which it cannot bear with patience or treat with dignity, which it must perchance leave to the irregular rule of a double foreigner, because it will not allow, under intelligible compromises, a portion of the English-speaking race to work out its own social problems by its own agencies? Is it not a problem worth solving, when, as we are told, the successful resistance to a contract rent which was an injustice, and now to an arbitrated rent which honestly endeavours to obviate an injustice, is so eating into the morality of the Irish people, that credit is almost a thing of the past, that traders live on ready money, that no one can trust his neighbour, and that mad newspapers are even striving to destroy public credit? These statements, freely made to me by Irishmen, are, it may be, exaggerations, but they must be probabilities.

More than twenty years ago, my distinguished friend Mr. Goldwin Smith, and I, as an humble fellow-worker with him, pointed out in the *Daily News* and *Star* newspapers how dangerous and demoralizing was the policy which Lord Palmerston's Government was pursuing with the colonies. At that time half the British army was in these dependencies, and every particle of British spirit was out of them. We insisted that political independence and responsibility should go together, and that no nation was worth keeping which would not or could not undertake its own defence. We were of course soundly rated for our presumption by the editors, but we can point to the present position of these colonies, and the close approach which they have made to the ideal which we strove at that time to set up, as a proof that the principles which we advocated were sound, and that we were really working for the unity of the Empire.

The political victory of Mr. Parnell's party is practically complete. It was a faction in the last Parliament, it is a power in this; and I notice with satisfaction that its language is infinitely more temperate than it was a twelvemonth ago. It is in the nature of things that a victorious party becomes, if fairly used, always moderate. Its leaders say, and say, I make no doubt, with truth, that they do not wish to ruin their country, still less to be at variance with their countrymen. They can afford to pass by the Bobadils of the Orange party. They know that they must make their arrangements

D

and negotiate their treaty with the British nation, and with one party only in it.

Ireland, in consequence of the unhappy schooling of centuries, is a nation without a policy, without parties; factions taking the place of parties, without responsibilities. All the charges which have been made against the Irish are simply tributes to the truth of what all genuine students of Irish history have to admit, that the faults of its present age are to be traced to its bringing-up. No child, spoilt at one time, severely chastised at another, has been educated in such a political nursery of caprice as Ireland has been. She has been debarred from having national leaders and a mature purpose, because it has been the constant practice to exclude the former from affairs and to thwart the latter.

The Scotch, after the accession of the House of Stuart, were treated as harshly by the English Government as the Irish were. Scotland had an aristocracy infinitely worse than the Irish was, even in its worst times. The religious persecution under which Ireland suffered during the existence of the Penal Code was gentleness itself when compared with the cruelties inflicted on the Scotch Presbyterians. To increase the bitterness of the Scotchman's lot, the worst cruelties were inflicted by men who had affected in their earlier days to sympathize with the national cause, the national religion; but who, turning renegade, became the familiars and executioners of that Scotch Inquisition which was established after the Restoration. Scotch trade was crippled as mercilessly by the English Parliament, for a century after the union of the crowns, as Irish trade was from the days of the Pensionary Parliament of the Restoration till the legislation of 1779. The Scottish union of 1706 was obtained by agencies as questionable as those which characterized the Irish union of 1800. It was, it must be admitted, followed by nearly as much discontent. The representation of the Scotch people in Parliament, up to 1832, was far more scandalous than that of England or Ireland. But the Scotch always remained a nation with definite ends and aims, though the political education of Scotland grew under all these difficulties. In the north of Scotland, where the patriarchal theory of tribal government had prevailed, the people suffered more wrongs than the Irish did. The Irish were, it is true, transferred from old lords to new ones, the latter being aliens to them in race and religion. But the Scottish clansman found that the father of his tribe became its tyrant when taught by the lawyers of Edinburgh how to turn his shadowy rights of headship into the highly advantageous status of a law-made landlord. I doubt whether the Irish ejections ever reached the cruelty and harshness of the Highland clearings. I know no ingratitude more callous than the conduct of those chieftains who repaid the devotion of their followers by the expatriation of their clansmen. It is true that there is plenty of discontent in Scotland, and that the discontent is taking a highly practical turn; but during the long age of oppression the Scottish nation has neither halted, nor lost place, nor lost heart, nor failed to make progress. For with all the faults of the Scotch administration, Scotland, even when misgoverned, was governed by her own children.

The problem before the English Parliament is not whether the claims of this or that party are to prevail, not whether the demands which I presume the Irish Nationalists will make should be conceded, not whether this or that interest should be guaranteed, protected, preserved; but how the scandalous, the intolerable reproach of the present condition of Ireland shall be removed or reformed, how Ireland shall be made capable of self-government, and be turned from hatred towards England into amity towards England. The problem must be solved, and solved early. We cannot, for our credit, now that the affairs of England are at last in the hands of the people of England, permit that the scandal of a poor, an angry, a rebellious nation should remain close to our doors.

To my mind the only solution of the problem, the only remedy for the scandal, is to be found in the transference of the responsibilities of self-government to those of the Irish people whom the Irish people may desire to trust their fortunes to. There is no question that the political unity of Ireland and Great Britain must continue. No reasonable person in Great Britain holds that Ireland should have entire political independence, the independence which was conceded in 1782. The experiment was tried, and failed. I suspect that most of the people who talk about Grattan's Parliament know very little of its history, less of its policy, least of all about the inherent vices of its constitution—vices which would reappear in 1886 as surely as they were manifest just about a century ago. Pitt took the precedent of the Scottish union, and would, but for the obstinacy of the King, have established as complete, or nearly as complete, a religious equality in Ireland as the Ministers of Queen Anne discovered or conceded in Scotland. Nor do I discover that any responsible Irishmen are demanding the political isolation of Ireland.

The nearest analogue to the reform of Irish abuses, and the development of political and social responsibility in Ireland, is the State of the American Union. The State in the Federal Constitution elects its head or governor, has its elective Senate and House of Representatives, possesses the power of enacting local laws and of imposing direct taxation on property, real and personal. It has its own police under its own management, and superintends the education of the young within its own boundaries, though this education is not sectarian; while it provides from its own resources the cost of this education, which is free. But it can impose no customs duty or excise; it can shelter no offender against the criminal law, and protect no citizen against civil process; it cannot have its own currency laws, but must submit to those of the Federal Union; it cannot have its own bankruptcy law; it has no authority whatever over army, navy, or militia; it has nothing to do with the national defence or with foreign policy; and it can decline no burdens which the authority of Congress imposes on it for federal purposes. The proceedings of the Federal Congress and the States representatives are liable to a double veto, direct and indirect; the former being that of the President and Governor, which may be overridden; the latter that of the Supreme Court, which decides on the question whether enactments are constitutional or not, and disallows them in the latter contingency. Most educated Americans believe that the power of the Supreme Court is very salutary. The exercise of this power is of course judicial, and is accompanied by reasons.

Now, in my opinion, something closely analogous to this constitution should be conferred on the Irish people. I am persuaded that the same sort of constitution should be given to Scotland, Wales, and North and South England. It exists in the United States, beause the early members of the Union were familiar with self-government, and had long elaborated its system before the War of Independence occurred. A system of local or State government has not been developed in England, though constitutional antiquaries are well aware that its construction would be merely the restoration of a system which is older than the monarchy, infinitely older than the two Houses of Parliament, and still more ancient than the unsatisfactory system of lords-lieutenant, county magistrates, and non-elective boards.

The establishment of such a local Parliament in Ireland, call it by what name you will, would instantly throw on the

Irish people the obligation and the responsibility of adjusting and harmonizing its whole social system. I decline to believe that were such a concession made, or rather such an act of duty and wisdom done, that Ireland would at once begin to commit political suicide. Instead of being ruled by others as hitherto, and of being consequently hostile to all government, it would have to rule itself, and consequently, by the law of self-preservation, would be forthwith loyal to government. Whether the work would be carried out by the present representatives of Irish discontent is a question the answer to which does not concern the inhabitants of Great Britain, but is a matter which may be entirely left to the Irish people. It is, however, clear that in politics the critical faculty is entirely different from the constructive faculty, and the latter will, in such a new state of things, be the needful quality. I do not remember that Mr. Parnell's followers have ever exhibited the slightest trace of any ability for constructive legislation, however highly their critical powers may have been developed, schooled, or manipulated.

Great dread is expressed about committing to the local and elected authorities in Ireland the management of their own police, with the duty, of course, of meeting as much of its cost as is imposed on English ratepayers. But the answer is, that if you diminish the powers of local self-government in matters entirely local, you diminish *pro tanto* that responsibility which is the crying defect in the local administration of Ireland. And if it be answered, that the Irish people, through their local representatives, would use their own police system as the training-ground for a national force, to be employed for seditious purposes and ultimately for a military struggle, the answer is twofold. First, the satisfaction of national aspirations and the concession of national responsibility would at once cut away the ground for that political discontent which manifests itself in political outrages and Fenian vapourings; for patriotic Irishmen, however wrong-headed, could hardly hate, and strive to overthrow by violence, the Government of their own choice. And next, the act would be as much an act of rebellion, to be put down peremptorily and instantly, as the attempt of an American State to organize an army or a militia, with the object of resistance to the Federal Government, would be.

Some rhetorical politicians have argued that concessions of self-government to Ireland should be accompanied by guarantees for the protection of certain kinds of property, and particularly the judicial rents, and for securing the rights, or even the existence, of the minority. Now, I can conceive nothing more dangerous to the minority than a guarantee of its rights or its existence. There is no reason to believe that the Irish minority will be sacrified, however provoking its attitude is, and however shallow and unreal is its claim to exceptional loyalty. But if the law tells the majority that it distrusts the intentions of the majority towards the minority, it suggests the policy which it intends to deprecate. One would have thought that by this time the value of legislative guarantees had been sufficiently discounted. When Dissenters were admitted to municipal rights they were compelled to declare or make oath that they would do nothing to weaken the influence of the Established Church. They accepted the condition, and answered it with an organization against the Establishment. Parliamentary guarantees are of the nature of promissory oaths, which have never secured what they aimed at—viz., loyalty to forms of government and reigning families, and that political orthodoxy which is supposed to be developed from religious conformity. Plenty of oaths were taken on behalf of James II., and few were kept. The early Hanoverian succession was girdled by promissory oaths, and yet no one accused Shippon and his Jacobite followers in the Commons with perjury.

The judicial rents must be left to the new and natural course of events. People absurdly talk about Parliamentary titles, and hint not obscurely that this makes the rent which issues from a parliamentary title a vested interest. But all that the Encumbered Estates Court gave was a clear title barring all prior claims. It no more guaranteed rents than the parliamentary title to railway stock guarantees dividends. Many of the purchasers under the courts doubled their rents, without having laid out a shilling on their new possessions. Some, as the Scotch say, "gat a gliff," and reversed their policy. But the landlord cannot get a rent when the produce of the tenant's little holding, however fertile his patch may be, does not come to more than the necessaries of life. He cannot get a rent if the holding is larger, but the value of its produce will only keep the tenant going and the land in heart. Hence the Irish Nationalists, with a true interpretation of the facts, insist on migration, and are opposed to emigration. Their action is certainly disinterested, for an expatriated and disaffected Irishman is a far more able and lavish contributor to the funds of the National League than any can be who win a scanty subsistence in the three southern provinces. They are also, in their contention, the best friends of the landlords; but it is certain that a fair-sized and prosperous homestead is a far better rent agency than a scanty and barren one can be. Nor can any one doubt that, however sacred rent may be, national and even personal existence are more sacred.

But I firmly believe that, with a wide and efficient system of self-government, all alarms will be found to be baseless. The most fertile field for ambitious and shallow demagogues is well-grounded discontent. The least hopeful prospect for them—and I am far from saying that Mr. Parnell and his followers are unpatriotic—is genuine responsibility, such as the obligation of managing the internal affairs of the Irish nation would be. One of the few wise things which Henry the Eighth said or did was his answer and action about the Gerald of his day. No one, he was told, in Ireland can govern the Gerald. Then said he, " Gerald is the man to govern Ireland." Ireland has chosen Mr. Parnell as its leader. I would give Ireland the opportunity of making him her Minister. It will be time to think of taking away from the Irish the rights of representative government when they have failed to carry out a workable form of local self-government.

On the lines which I have sketched the distribution of local and imperial taxation in Ireland is self-adjusting, just as those of an American State and of the Federal Government are. If Ireland undertakes the management of her internal affairs, she must pay the cost of her own machinery. To claim the assistance of England in this necessary duty is mendicancy, and should be repudiated, not only in the interest of the English taxpayer, but as dangerous to Irish self-respect and genuine independence. But while the imperial revenue from Ireland, levied on precisely the same lines as in England and Scotland, and collected by the officers of the Empire, should go into the imperial exchequer, the defences of Ireland, its harbours, those of its public charges which are part of the machinery of international police and international duty, its contingent of the army, the militia, and the debt, should be, must be, under imperial control and maintained from the imperial exchequer.

JAMES E. THOROLD ROGERS.

ALFRED RUSSEL WALLACE, LL.D.

IT is a fundamental principle of true Liberalism, that every distinct nationality or separate community has a right to be governed in whatever manner it thinks best. This principle may sometimes be in abeyance—in the case of conquered or subject nations who are different in race from their conquerors and lower in the scale of civilization, or in that of colonies or partially settled territories which are either not sufficiently homogeneous or sufficiently populous to render local self-government practicable or even desirable —but for all distinct nationalities who are in the same scale of civilization as their rulers the principle is fully applicable, and Liberals invariably applaud every claim of such peoples for self-government, while they as invariably condemn as tyrannous and unjust the refusal to comply with their demands by any more powerful Government which may have held the claimants in subjection. Our sympathy was given to Greece in its rebellion against Turkey; to Hungary when demanding a national government from Austria; to Italy when fighting to free Naples, Rome, and Milan, and to establish Italian unity; and we now give our best wishes to the Bulgarians in their earnest struggle for union under one free and national Government. And in every case in which it has been fairly tried among a nearly homogeneous people the result has been satisfactory; peace, progress, and contentment taking the place of ever-recurring revolt and chronic discontent.

Liberal opinion being thus so uniformly favourable to the claims of any distinct European nationality to freedom and self-government, it is surely inconsistent for Liberals not to be equally favourable to the claims of Ireland. The case is not, it is true, exactly comparable to that of any of those we have just referred to, but in the eyes of an unprejudiced observer the difference is all in favour of the sister isle. The Irish are a distinct race, with a national history, language, and literature of their own. They differ from us in religion. They have been ruled by us as a conquered nation for many centuries, and they have never ceased to claim and to struggle for their freedom. It is true that the tyranny and oppression which we so long exercised in Ireland is now a thing of the past, but the form of representative government which we have given them is not a reality, because Irishmen are necessarily a minority in the British Parliament; and so great are the prejudices of a conquering race and a hostile religion, that to this day Catholic Ireland is ruled by English rather than by Irish ideas, and by means of Englishmen and Protestants, instead of by Irishmen and Catholics. Such a government, even if good in itself, can never be acceptable to the people governed. We have now by an extended franchise given Ireland the opportunity of declaring its wishes. It has decided almost unanimously that it demands self-government, not as an independent State, but as an integral part of the British Empire; and to refuse this demand is to abandon the first and most essential principle of true Liberalism. At the same time, self-preservation is a primary law of nature for States as for individuals, and we are perfectly justified in insisting upon such a real and effective union of the two countries under the Supreme Government as shall conduce to the stability and peace of the United Kingdom. But with this proviso the demand of Ireland for internal self-government should be granted freely and unreservedly. Thus alone shall we be able to satisfy the just expectations of the Irish people ; thus alone shall we secure their friendship and respect, and in no distant future find in Ireland a source of national strength, instead of being, as hitherto, a constant thorn in our side and a perpetual drain upon our resources.

There are, however, two special sources of difficulty in Ireland which require to be considered before we can determine upon the lines within which we may allow complete self-government. These are, of course, religion and landlordism. The Roman Catholic religion prevails over by far the larger part of Ireland ; but in the north-east, and especially in the four counties of Londonderry, Antrim, Down, and Armagh, Protestants of a very pronounced type form the bulk of the population. These counties have shown their wish to remain under direct English rule by returning almost exclusively Conservative members to the present Parliament ; and exactly the same Liberal principles which compel us to grant self-government to the great bulk of the Irish people forbid us to force these northern districts into a union which is repulsive to them, and which would inevitably lead to extreme dissatisfaction and perhaps even to civil war.

That it is the only true policy to allow populations, separated from their neighbours by religion, race, or local prejudice, to decide for themselves under what Government they wish to live, is well illustrated by the example of the Canadian Dominion. At first, British Columbia and Prince Edward's Island declined to join the four united provinces, but a few years later they voluntarily entered the Dominion ; while Newfoundland still remains a separate colony. Happily, neither England nor Canada seeks to force this small colony to unite with its neighbours, and it is not alleged that evil results have followed this course ; while it is almost certain that at some future time the union will be voluntarily made. In like manner, if the Protestant and Conservative portion of Ulster is now permitted to choose its own form of government, all the difficulties arising from a forced union will be avoided : while it is not improbable that in course of time the antagonism that now prevails may die out, and the desire to form part of a United Ireland lead to an ultimate voluntary union.

The other difficulty arises from the fact that the land of Ireland is largely owned by Englishmen or by absentees; that the people have been subjected to much oppression by landlords or by their agents, and have been often evicted to make room for new tenants or to form extensive grazing farms; and that there is still a prevalent wish to get rid of landlords altogether, and to establish a peasant proprietary over the whole country. It is therefore feared that an Irish Parliament will endeavour to obtain the land for the people, either without payment to existing landlords, or with altogether inadequate compensation.

It cannot be said, however, that the representatives of the Irish National party have given any reason to suppose that they would sanction such a course, while many of them have openly advocated the purchase of the land at its fair value. It must be remembered that a considerable number of the Irish members are themselves landowners; that besides the great landlords there are a large number of others who have comparatively small estates and are mostly residents; and that any general scheme of confiscation would receive so much opposition and lead to such disastrous consequences that it would hardly be attempted. But if there may be supposed to be any danger of such unjust legislation, it would be rendered impossible by the power of veto, which, as in the case of all our colonies, is retained by the Crown, and which, if any attempt were made to confiscate the property of

British subjects, would certainly be exercised. It may also be urged that to assert beforehand that we know the Irish Parliament will make a bad use of its power, is to repeat the universal plea of the despot who denies freedom to his subjects. Experience shows us that newly enfranchised peoples do not usually make a bad use of their liberty. They are in most cases very anxious to justify themselves in the eyes of other nations, and are careful not to prove themselves unfit for freedom by entering on a course of legislation which would be repugnant to every civilized Government. We shall only condemn ourselves if we declare our belief that seven centuries of English rule has so debased the Irish character that her people are not fitted to enjoy that measure of self-government which Bulgarians and Servians, but newly released from Turkish misrule, have shown themselves well qualified for, and by which they have already so greatly benefited.

Having thus laid down the general principles which should guide us in approaching the question of Irish self-government, it remains only to indicate in what manner it may best be brought about, and what limitations, if any, we should impose upon its exercise.

In determining these points we find valuable precedents in the history of the Canadian Dominion. Nearly half a century ago, both Upper and Lower Canada were driven into actual rebellion by somewhat similar causes to those which excite dissatisfaction in Ireland—the action of an executive, appointed by the English Government, in opposition to the wishes of the people. From the time when free representative institutions were granted to the people of Canada all such troubles were at an end. Other difficulties arose, however, from the union of the two Canadian provinces, which differed fundamentally in race and religion; Lower Canada being mostly French and Roman Catholic, while Upper Canada was English and Protestant. The antagonism of these two parties often led to disputes and to a dead-lock in the government, which their separation under the Dominion, with the free control of their internal affairs, has completely set at rest. We have here a most important lesson as to the impolicy of attempting to force any considerable population into a union which is opposed either to its racial or religious prejudices.

The great success which has attended the federal union of the several Canadian provinces invites us to consider how this success has been attained; and we find that we may fairly impute it to our having thrown upon the provinces to be united the responsibility of determining the limits of provincial and federal authority. Delegates from the several provinces settled the details and determined the precise terms of the Act of Union, and Lord Carnarvon, the then Colonial Secretary, bore testimony to the statesman-like qualities which were displayed in the settlement of sectional difficulties, the unravelling of knotty points, the mutual forbearance, and the zeal and assiduity displayed during the prolonged sittings of the conference. When the Bill, thus carefully elaborated, was introduced into Parliament by Lord Carnarvon, it was received with approbation by all parties, and passed through all its stages in both Houses of Parliament in less than a month.

If now we consider that in this case there were antagonisms of race and of religion hardly less pronounced than those between Ireland and England or between Catholic Ireland and Presbyterian Ulster, that two of the provinces had been in rebellion against the mother country, and that the smaller colonies which were included in the union had many sectional jealousies and local prejudices, it seems probable that the scheme which finally harmonized all these conflicting elements will afford the surest guide in our endeavours to formulate a system of union between Ireland and England. It is true that some of the Irish Nationalists claim the larger amount of independence which we have granted to our various colonies, but the more moderate among them have indicated that of the separate provinces of the Canadian Dominion as the minimum they are prepared to accept. If now the Liberal party adopt this same amount of self-government as indicating in general terms the maximum they are prepared to grant, a common basis of negotiation will be established, and there will assuredly be no difficulty in agreeing upon the details of a Bill which, if frankly supported by the whole body of Irish Nationalists and English Liberals, can be carried by an overwhelming majority in the House of Commons, and will therefore, after a struggle, be passed by the Upper House.

The Act establishing the Dominion of Canada gives to the people of each province the complete control of everything pertaining to their internal affairs, subject only to their allegiance to a common sovereign, and their duties as members of the British Empire ; while the Federal Government (which in the case of Ireland would be the Parliament of the United Kingdom) enacts all the laws in which the whole community have a common interest, such as those relating to trade and commerce, navigation, fisheries, indirect and direct taxation, postage, and criminal law. Taking this division of functions as a guiding principle, the problem is how to apply it in the case of Ireland, and it is certain that a satisfactory result will never be reached by the method hitherto adopted in all special legislation for that country, that of carefully avoiding direct consultation with the representatives of the Irish people.

The obvious course seems to be for the British Government (which I assume to be a Liberal one) to appoint a body of delegates to meet an equal number of delegates appointed by the Irish Nationalist representatives, in order to draw up a Bill establishing self-government for Ireland on the basis of the relation of a Canadian province to the Dominion. Points of difficulty should be referred back to the general body of Irish representatives, and to the English Ministry, so that when finally settled the Bill may be carried through Parliament without needing substantial alteration.

At the same time (or before, if possible), a Bill establishing a very broad system of local self-government in the three kingdoms should be brought forward, and this having been carried, the determination of the exact mode of Irish representation in the House of Commons would be greatly facilitated. The usual objection, that if English members take no part in legislation for Ireland, it would be unfair to allow Irish members to interfere in English legislation, would cease to have any weight, because all (or almost all) the powers of self-government given to Ireland as a whole (except Protestant Ulster) would be also given to the counties, or larger divisions of England, Wales, and Scotland; and the Imperial Government would in future have to deal only with matters affecting the external relations of the country at large, or with those branches of legislation expressly excepted from the scope of the Irish Parliament or the English councils. Parliamentary legislation would henceforth be essentially British and Imperial, and in such a Parliament Ireland would have a just claim to her full share of representation, while some of her best men should form part of every British Ministry.

Whether the Irish Parliament should consist of the same men who are chosen to sit at Westminster, or should form a distinct body, is a question that purely concerns the Irish people, and should be left for them to decide. There would evidently be many advantages in having only one body of representatives. The best men in the country would be available for the home government, and they would certainly learn something by experience gained in the British Parliament. The office of representative would rise in importance and dignity, while members of the two Parliaments would more fully realize their responsibility, and be less likely to rush into hasty and ill-considered legislation. It would be easy to arrange the sittings of the Irish Parliament so as not to interfere with ours, and it must be remembered that when all local affairs are settled by local authorities, the sessions of the Imperial Legislature will not require to be nearly so long or so laborious as they are now. This matter is, however, essentially one that Ireland should decide for herself, and no attempt should be made to interfere with her free decision as to the numbers and qualifications of the members constituting her domestic Legislature.

In thus endeavouring to point out what should be the attitude of the Liberal party towards Ireland at the present crisis I have aimed at formulating principles rather than discussing details. Above all things, it seems to me necessary that Liberals should justify the appellation they have chosen for themselves by approaching the consideration of this momentous question in a spirit of sympathy for the aspirations of the Irish people, and of true charity in avoiding imputations of bad motives or predictions of inevitable failure. If we do this honestly and fearlessly, we shall reap our reward in the establishment, for the first time in history, of a really United Kingdom of Great Britain and Ireland.

ALFRED R. WALLACE.

ANNA BATESON.

IT would have been well for the world had the fact always been borne in mind that nations have a good deal of human nature about them, just as individuals have.

If you wish to win regard, you must earn it by bestowing regard.

Those who are treated with contempt, suspicion, and dislike, will be sure to repay your bad opinion by showing you the worst side of their character. Those who are never permitted to act for themselves must in the end become helpless.

These are mere truisms as between man and man; but no attempt is made to apply these natural principles as between nations.

For this neglect of common-sense diplomacy must take the chief share of blame.

Indeed, there are few features in modern political development more promising than the decay which has overtaken the business of diplomatists, with all their paraphernalia of State secrets, hidden schemes, and dark intrigue.

To the minds of crafty Ministers managing affairs in the olden time any course of action which was simple carried its own condemnation on its very face.

To begin with, their own vanity could not be flattered by any course which was simple and straightforward. They must, above all things, exhibit their own cleverness; they must shine, they must outwit the rival statesmen of the neighbouring country. Peace and goodwill among men were almost impossible while this went on, and while the people were kept in the dark and only treated like so many puppets at the pleasure of the wire-pulling rulers.

All this is changed. At the present day " the people " are to the front; and the golden rule of doing as you would be done by has some chance of being attended to.

Now, the first thing we have to do when we have injured our neighbour, and are convinced of our error, is frankly to admit that we have been wrong. This is the first step, and it should be taken before any other can succeed.

There have been signs lately, not a few, of a new and remarkable awakening of the English conscience in regard to the sister isle.

Sad to say, we have been roused from our ignorant apathy by terrible events, by outrage and crime.

These things have not terrorized us, but they have educated us.

We have been stirred to ask what are the causes leading to such dire results, and our complacency has been shaken.

It was instructive to watch during the recent election addresses how wide of their mark fell the words of candidates appealing to their audiences for power to quell Irish faction.

Silence for the most part, sometimes murmurs, scarcely ever anything like hearty applause, greeted such appeals; they fell flat.

A leaven has begun to work in the minds of our people, and it is by no means impossible that they may take up the question of Irish wrongs, as they have from time to time taken up popular movements in countries more remote. Why should we know or care so little about Ireland, the misgovernment of which lies directly at our own door, while we can stir the land from end to end on the subject of "Bulgarian atrocities," and the like? Read the history of Ireland as governed by us, and you will there find atrocities enough to stir your blood. That the Irish people have not been utterly crushed shows they must be made of tough fibre and have an indomitable spirit.

It is much to be wished that public meetings may be held and persons competent to the task invited to deliver addresses on Irish history and Irish affairs.

This is to be wished, not merely for the purpose of instructing and arousing our people, but with the practical object of making Irish demands more reasonable than they otherwise might be. This would be the probable result if we made it clear that our sympathies had been stirred. The spirit of hatred on their part would be assuaged, and they would see many things in a dispassionate way.

It has been said by some that whatever scheme of Home Rule may be decided on, it should at any rate be the work of our Parliament—it must be of our devising. This is exactly contrary to the principles of human nature.

If we make the best of schemes, and give it ready-made—impose it in fact, upon any set of people—is it not an every-day experience that they will be dissatisfied with it?

Let them make their own proposals, not only because they understand their own needs best, but because they will be satisfied with less when allowed a free hand.

Recalling the suggestion, that what holds good between man and man should be applied as between nations, it is startling to see how entirely this principle is ignored by those who assert (and their name is Legion) that the Irish are unfit to govern themselves, and must be treated like children.

Can there be an instance of more unparalleled impertinence?

Does our neighbour ask our leave before he holds the

key of his own door? Is it ours to give or to withhold? Let English people reflect how they would relish such language applied to themselves, and they can then realize how astoundingly insolent is its nature. Besides, we are here on the horns of a dilemma. Either the Irish are of a different race from ourselves and therefore not easily amenable to our methods of treatment, or they are of the same blood as the English, in which case they have the same virtues and vices as we have.

Coming to the practical question, how far we ought to go in the Home Rule direction, many excellent friends of Ireland draw the line sharply against absolute separation, and I would speak with great hesitation on a matter so momentous. But it is very seriously to be recollected that the first thing we have to do, the great object of the whole movement, is to satisfy the Irish people as a whole. If they were approached in a right spirit, it is almost certain they would see how much they have to lose by entire separation, and that their general feeling would be against it.

But to set up again a standard of direct prohibition might be full of risk. By fixing an arbitrary limit to the field of discussion we should probably give shape to a danger which has no life in it while let alone.

The grand point is to remove the hatred of England, which is the irritating cause why separation is hinted at; then let things shape themselves without fresh fetters. To remove the "irritating cause" we must of course deal with the landlords.

Volumes have been written, and doubtless will continue to be poured forth, as to the difficulties which beset this matter.

Of one thing we may rest assured—viz., that the old adage says truly, "There can be no omelette without breaking of eggs."

Where a great wrong, which has been done and backed up by us for generations, has to be set right, somebody must suffer.

In English society much lamentation is heard over the woes of the Irish landlords, and no doubt they are in a grievous plight.

But it is strange to see how society takes to heart the distress of Lord A. or Mrs. B., when it remained comparatively untouched by the intense wretchedness of the oppressed poor, whose voices went wailing up by thousands.

The landlords have had their good things, and they should be prepared for vicissitudes in the value of their possessions, as other holders of property have to take their chance of rise and fall.

It is expedient that a class shall suffer rather than a people perish.

If we feel that we cannot allow all the loss to fall on these unfortunate landowners, we must make up our minds to bear a part of the burden ourselves. Even supposing that for this cause we were forced to bear an extra tax for some years to come, the money would be better spent than many a million we ungrudgingly pay for wars we might well keep out of.

Moreover, a goodly sum would be saved us which we now have to spend on keeping up the military reinforcements in Ireland. What a relief it will be when we get rid of the shame and horror of seeing those reinforcements maintained there!

Visiting Dublin a year or two ago, I felt ashamed to speak with English tongue to the people while one saw the city held, like a foreign fortress, by our soldiers endlessly parading and flaunting our authority in the face of the population. Travelling about the country one had the chance of hearing expressions of feeling which were too general and too emphatic to be misunderstood.

Again, a shame and a horror it was to hear the Government spoken of as "the English Government," just as the Italians refused thirty years ago to accept the Austrian rule as other than extraneous. Widespread gloom and dissatisfaction were everywhere visible.

Amid the lovely scenery of Connemara, and even in Killarney, where English visitors, spending money freely, might help to make our country popular, it was impossible to feel happy or at ease.

It is only fair to say that there was a brighter side to the picture in the more loyal tone which appeared to prevail at Queenstown. A part of the Channel Fleet was lying there under the command of the Duke of Edinburgh, and no ill-feeling could be detected.

Possibly the pomp and beauty of the noble array appealed to the hearts of the beholders as a thing which was theirs as well as ours; here we could feel a common pride. The fleet lay there for no purpose of intimidation, and certainly the sight was one which could hardly fail to be appreciated by a glory-loving and imaginative people. "Home Rulers, marm! They can't show us the aqual of that now," said our boatman with a good-humoured twinkle in his eye.

It was with a certain feeling of anxiety that one heard the strains of the National Anthem float upon the air, played by the band at night; but no groans, no hissings were raised. Truly the Irish care more to be entitled to their own self-respect than they do for a share in the kingdoms of the world and the glory of them. But here, in the imperial department, they can share the glory without forfeiting their self-respect, and we have an excellent opportunity of attaching them on that side.

The thought occurred to the mind, that Irish lads might be among the handsome well-disciplined young fellows on board those vessels. What a change from their desolate homes on the bogside! and what a cheering thing to know that they need not feel they had forfeited their birthright for a mess of pottage, nor sold themselves body and soul, away from their people at home, away from love of country!

We have much to work upon, if we only knew how to apply it; if we only had the sense to lead these people, whom we cannot drive.

Love is better than hate; union is stronger than schism.

But without freedom there can be no love, no strength, no union.

The above fragmentary reflections have, I am aware, very little value. At any time but this they could hardly be worth uttering at all. But the Irish Question is in the air; the interest in it is confined to no party. All are beginning to perceive that something must be done, and the words of the humblest may find a hearing if sincerely spoken.

Asked at very short notice to give written expression to sentiments which I have held for many years past, I did not feel inclined to shrink from the responsibility. Also the desire is strong within me to express thankfulness at having lived to see this stir in the public mind.

Home Rule! How one can look back through long years to the time when the mere mention of any such project was the signal for derision!

Fenians were looked upon as the most visionary as well as the wickedest of men. When they threatened to make reprisals, their warnings were ridiculed habitually in the

English newspapers, and described as mere brag and bluster.

To call these things to mind does one's heart good.

It seems as if nothing need be despaired of, as if words of hope need never be empty words, not even when they echo the forlorn old cry of "GOD SAVE IRELAND!"

ANNA BATESON.

CHARLES BRADLAUGH, M.P.

THE fact that after six months of office the Conservative Ministry faces Parliament with the resignation both of its Lord Lieutenant and of its Chief Secretary for Ireland, is of the most vital gravity. The condition of Ireland was, as late as November, declared, in nearly every Conservative election speech, to be better under Lord Carnarvon's mild and conciliatory rule than it had ever been under Lord Spencer or his predecessor. In the autumn, Lord Randolph Churchill repeatedly stated that since 1883 crime in Ireland had been steadily diminishing—that he was not aware that there was any abnormal distress; and then in September he told us that after careful and sustained attention he had been unable to detect any sign of anything which was likely to occur in Ireland for which the powers of the ordinary law were not sufficient. Now Tory government in Ireland has suddenly utterly collapsed, and the Conservative Lord Lieutenant and his Chief Secretary are both abandoning their posts. The statement that Lord Carnarvon originally took office for a limited period only aggravates the case, for when Lord Salisbury after the election determined to continue in office, he should have at once arranged to fill the Lord Lieutenancy before any public knowledge of the resignation of Lord Carnarvon had agitated and unsettled the public mind. There is not even the pretence made, that Sir W. Hart Dyke's appointment was temporary. The fact is, the Tories have bought the

Irish vote at the election by vague promises which they dare not formulate into legislative proposals. Mr. Parnell's friends have, on his express orders, given their votes throughout England for Tories against Radicals, and now the Tories, unable to pay the understood price, cannot cope with the increased and increasing gravity of the crisis in Ireland.

The Irish difficulty must be honestly faced and boldly dealt with, and renewal of coercion must not be permitted. Exceptional legislation of a repressive character only perpetuates secret combination for armed and cowardly resistance : it does not cure or even lessen the evil, it only compels it to hide. Ireland is entitled to local self-government; so are Scotland, England, and Wales. It is said that any large and generous measure of self-government for Ireland means separation from Great Britain. It has not meant it in Canada, though the temptations from the United States have often been great. It has not meant it in our Australasian colonies, though the strain has sometimes been severe. It need not mean it—it ought not to mean it—in Ireland. A grave difficulty for earnest peace-loving Radicals is, that we do not know what measure of Home Rule is now asked for by, or would content, the Irish party led by Mr. Parnell. Speeches have been made about the restoration of Grattan's Parliament, modified by the absence of the House of Peers; but Grattan's Protestant Parliament, with election by limited suffrage, is dead and gone. Mr. Isaac Butt did formulate a scheme, and the English would have been wise if, sixteen years ago, they had met Mr. Butt even more than half-way. Radicals should ask Mr. Parnell to state exactly the ground he takes, and should insist on a clear and speedy answer. Some months ago it was generally supposed that he would have been satisfied with the scheme of local and national councils propounded by Mr. Chamberlain. It is difficult, and it may be impossible, to get any satisfactory solution of the Irish problem, unless at least there is reasonable frankness on the part of those guiding Irish feeling. Englishmen ought to be very generous in their Irish legislation, for it is unfortunately too true that much of the enduring discontent amongst all Roman Catholic Irishmen is the result of generations of misgovernment of Ireland in which all English parties are guilty.

Irishmen wielding influence should remember that it is the interest of all who love Ireland to close this horrible crisis as rapidly as possible. At present all mercantile enterprise, all agricultural endeavour, is arrested in Ireland by the uncertainty of the future, and the sadness and mischief of the present.

The political organizations in Ireland have, since 1879, succeeded, in Leinster, Munster, and Connaught, in utterly disorganizing the machinery of government, but the means used are nearly all destructive of future as well as of present well-being. Moonlighting and boycotting have, in one form or another, been present in Ireland for nearly two hundred years—they demoralize those who take part in them, those who encourage, those who acquiesce. If Mr. Parnell could convene a purely Irish Parliament in Dublin to-morrow, his task would be no easy one even to control those with whom he has secretly worked during the past eight years. I would support the widest measure of self-government in Ireland which did not involve the destruction of the nation of which I am a citizen. I would have Ireland in the United Kingdom what Massachusetts is in the United States.

If there is to be a one-chamber Parliament or Council sitting in Ireland, it will of course necessitate, in the statute creating it, provisions in the nature of a Constitution, such as now exists in each State of the American Union, with a Supreme Court created with power to declare the invalidity of any statute exceeding the powers given by the Constitution. What law-making powers do Irishmen seek? There cannot be two supreme Parliaments. How do Irishmen propose to deal with taxation? What arrangements do they suggest as to apportionment of the National Debt? To what extent do they propose to contribute to the cost of the army and navy? Do they claim only one Parliament for all Ireland? or one for the three provinces of Leinster, Connaught, and Munster, and a second for Ulster? If they say the minority in Ulster should give way to the majority in Ireland, why do they contend that the minority in Ireland should not give way to the majority in the United Kingdom?

It is impossible to ignore the intense and active hostility which has hitherto prevailed in Ireland between the Orangemen and Roman Catholics. What reason is there to suppose that under one Dublin Parliament this hostility —which has kept bitterly alive since the battle of the Boyne—will now die away?

That Mr. Parnell and his friends may do much mischief to their own country and to ours by prolonging the struggle is beyond dispute, but they can do no good to themselves. It is the interest of Englishmen to end a state of things which is a disgrace to civilization, and the effort must be fearlessly and practically made by English Radicals, even if Mr. Parnell will not help us with friendly counsel and kindly hearing. The great leaders of the Liberals, who have for months been discussing this question, should at once state in Parliament the measure they think just. The Radicals are not yet strong enough to carry any great Irish measure by themselves; but the Whigs and Liberals can do nothing at the next general election if the Radicals be hostile. If Mr. Gladstone, Mr. Chamberlain, and other men to whom we look for guidance, will now be frank and outspoken, they may save the nation from much misery and dishonour. The best solution would probably be one which would equally give to England, Ireland, Scotland, and Wales, by County Boards and National Councils, the free and full administration of all such of their local affairs as did not involve imperial interests. If, however, this task be too great for immediate enterprise, the Irish question must not wait. Justice must be fully done, and as we do it murder and outrage must be stopped or punished. Irish leaders could stay it somewhat, if they would. At present, I fear, they rather use language which promotes it. Our past has taught them that we have been amenable to fear, when we have been deaf to prayer. Surely it is time to end this crime and shame.

CHARLES BRADLAUGH.

REV. R. ACLAND ARMSTRONG.

THE consideration of the great Irish problem must be dominated by the fact that we have deliberately consulted the Irish people. Knowing all that we knew, we deliberately created such a franchise, and so distributed the seats to be filled, that, for the first time in history, the mass of the Irish population should be able to utter their voice in constitutional fashion. This was our own act, and by its result we must abide.

The result is this : Sixteen members are sent to Parliament from the Scottish settlement round Lough Neagh to support the Conservative party. Two more Conservatives join them from Dublin University. Every other constituency in Ireland, scornfully ignoring Conservative and Liberal alike, votes Nationalist. Where opposition is ventured, its rout is so overwhelming as only to emphasize the extraordinary unity of the national sentiment. Irish Ireland, by us deliberately consulted, replies with the unanimous demand for Home Rule.

To go, with Earl Cowper, behind this fact, and pretend that the national vote means something other than it says, is to make an insidious attack on the fundamental principle of representative institutions. The constitution knows no other mode of ascertaining the wish of the constituencies than to take their vote.

The claim is no longer, then, the claim of Mr. Parnell or of a party. It is the claim of Ireland. The behaviour of any group of men in former Parliaments, the tactics of any politician in the electoral campaign, form no legitimate item in the problem. That problem is how to treat a national demand for the first time authoritatively made.

The demand is for Home Rule. It is too late to suggest, with Mr. Trevelyan, departmental boards, by way of educating the people in self-government. Measures which at the right time would have been statesmanlike, may, when the moment is past, be no better than quackery. Such a proposal in the late Parliament would have shown political genius; now it betrays inadequate conception of the situation. Ireland has claimed Home Rule.

We may treat that claim thus. We may say that we have made a mistake in continuing to Ireland any share in our parliamentary institutions—that she requires for her own sake, or ours, to be governed from above. We may remove her representatives from Westminster, garrison all her towns, and hold her down. There would be a certain statesmanship in such a course. It would be self-consistent. It would liberate England for the moment from an overwhelming embarrassment; it would restore order in Ireland. The objections are that it would be a reversal of all our political traditions, that the British electorate would never sanction it, and that it would be incomparably wicked.

Our second possible course is to continue to govern Ireland by force while still maintaining constitutional forms. The objection is, that such a political hypocrisy must fail in the future as it has failed in the past—must fail more than ever now, because the hypocrisy would be patent instead of veiled. Such a policy must be with or without coercion. If with, the English conscience can know no peace, while Irish intrigue can only be fomented. If without, the anarchy which covers Ireland at the present moment must be chronic. It is easy to expatiate on the dangers and drawbacks involved in any course; it would be difficult to find in any course dangers and drawbacks surpassing those involved in the *status quo*.

Our third possible course is to accord such a measure of Home Rule as shall satisfy the Irish demand. The limits within which such a measure must be framed are, on the one side, free scope for the Irish to manage their own internal affairs; on the other, the maintenance of the connection with the Crown. It is no business of the British electorate to define more particularly than that. It is for the mass of citizens to decree the general direction of a policy in accordance with their views of justice and expediency; it is for the skilled statesmen whom they employ to construct particular measures embodying the national mandate.

The concession of Home Rule, like every other course, has its dangers and its drawbacks; unlike any other, it is inherently just, and affords hope of a union between England and Ireland—not in form, but in fact. It may mean misgovernment in Ireland, but cannot mean such serious misgovernment as Ireland has received from us. The alternation of concession and coercion is the most demoralizing mode of government practised on this earth. It may mean misgovernment in Ireland; but do they who think so remember the sobering effect of responsibility on politicians? It is one thing to behave extravagantly as a member of a small and hated minority in an alien Parliament, another thing to behave extravagantly as a responsible legislator in the Parliament of one's own country. Many a man votes for that while in a powerless minority which he would never vote for in an effective majority

The cry that we have already made concessions enough to Ireland confounds indulgence with justice. Ireland asks no concessions. She asks leave to carry her own burden and control her own economy. To be free and hungry is better than to be in bonds well-fed. To self-respect it is no consolation that the despot means well. No favouritism can compensate a nation for the forfeiture of her autonomy. And what favouritism we have shown to Ireland has been, like all favouritism, capricious. We have invented boons for her; but while the representations of the Scotch members have always been respectfully received and generally acceded to without demur, no such recognition has habitually been accorded to the united voice of the Irish members. It is beyond question that *if* the Irish people sincerely desire to develop their manufactures, their fisheries, their internal communications, their external commerce, an Irish Parliament would carry out that desire with ten times the celerity and not one-tenth of the friction with which the Imperial Parliament will do so.

If misunderstandings, jealousies, hatreds between its parts, imperil in any degree the integrity of an empire, if goodwill, respect, and sympathy in any degree consolidate it, then the integrity of this British Empire will become incomparably more secure on the not distant day on which the Irish Parliament is opened on College Green.

The legislative union was an experiment: it has failed. The restoration of an Irish legislative chamber will deserve the name of revolution just as much and just as little as its abolition eighty years ago, and by no means so much as the tremendous constitutional changes of the past two sessions.

The establishment of Home Rule in Ireland is expedient in the interests of English legislation. No Rules of Procedure can render Parliament an efficient legislative organism, while in its membership it comprises eighty Irishmen burning with a sense of intolerable wrong, and backed by the moral support of a nation. Laws of debate strong enough to suppress them will be strong enough to suppress English liberties as well. The cry for vengeance which too many Liberals have raised against Mr. Parnell can only be gratified by a course which will stifle all that is noblest in the aspirations of the Liberalism of Great Britain. Defiance of Ireland means the paralysis of politics in England. Those Englishmen who make light of the expression of opinion delivered by the Irish people, make light of the spirit of that constitution which is the bulwark of their own freedom.

Amid the Babel of political passion and the labyrinth of political intrigue, he will do best who most steadfastly stands by the conviction that the just course is always the wise course; and that politician will show himself in the present crisis the most sterling statesman who most boldly shapes his measures to the demands of justice. The genius of such a statesman will know how to reconcile the satisfaction of Irish aspiration with the welfare of the whole people of these islands. One such statesman we possess, and for his word we wait.

R. ACLAND ARMSTRONG.

WILFRID SCAWEN BLUNT.

MY views on the Irish Question have already been made public; but at a crisis, such as the present is, I am happy to restate them.

They are based upon a principle very generally admitted, and whose truth I recognize as of universal application— namely, that nations are the best judges of their own affairs, and have an inherent right, subject only to the rights of their neighbours, to self-government. In considering the case of Ireland I have only therefore to ask myself, first, whether the Irish are in fact a nation; and secondly, whether Home Rule for them would imply a wrong to ourselves.

With regard to the first, I have no difficulty in coming to a decision. If history shows anything, it is that the Celtic Irish are as distinct from our Anglo-Norman selves as the Basques are from the Spaniards, the Arabs from the Turks, the Hungarians from the Germans. They have hardly anything in common with us except their language, and even that is an accident of modern date. In their instincts of race, political traditions, and social prejudices, they stand a whole world apart from us; and on some points they seem to belong to another age and another epoch of development from our own. It is the refusal to understand this that has caused all attempts at fusion, even the most honest, on our part, to fail; and the past shows nothing in our relations with Ireland but a succession of unwise endeavours to turn Irishmen into Englishmen, alternating with savage outbreaks of disappointment when we have recognised its impossibility. The Celtic Irish, however, though more than once on the point of extinction, have shown a surprising vitality through the past centuries, and have over and over again absorbed their conquerors; and they are now once more asserting themselves, as doggedly bent as ever on following their own way and scorning our conception of their interests. Whatever may be their numerical proportion to the whole population of the island, it is certain that they have imbued five-sixths of it with their ideas and hopes and political aspirations, and that they stand out distinctly as united in their demand for Home Rule. Moreover, it is abundantly evident that the Irish problem of to-day is not in its nature different from what it has always been. We have to choose for the twentieth time between withdrawing our garrison and effecting a re-conquest. There is no middle course. For myself, of course, I cannot doubt which is the policy which justice bids us pursue. I cannot see that we have any business with re-conquest, and I am clear that for Ireland her own way is best.

We owe, however, doubtless—and this is the second point—a duty to ourselves in the matter which we cannot overlook. Our connection with Ireland is a fact of seven centuries' standing, and cannot lightly be broken. If it were true, as some pretend, that Home Rule there would ruin us commercially, or expose us to foreign invasion, we should be obliged to dare even injustice in our self-defence. But I confess I see no such danger. It seems to me a wholly false analogy to compare our position towards Ireland with that of America towards the

Southern States. The Southern States, had they established their independence, would have forced the American Republic into an attitude of permanent armed defence on the Western Continent which they were justified in refusing. But with us the sole military effect of such Home Rule as the Irish now demand would be to release us in war time from the embarrassment of occupying a disaffected province always ready to hail an invader. A great deal of nonsense is talked about Ireland being too close to our shores to admit of any risks of attack from that quarter. But people seem to forget that we have lived for centuries quite as close to France, and that Ireland is far more likely to invite our enemies now to help her than she would be to join in an attack if we gave her what she asked. The Irish are not a maritime nation, and, separated by the sea, never could be a danger to us, were they ever so ill-disposed. The danger is, in our present position, of holding them down by force on their own ground.

There remains the danger to our pockets, and this is a matter for economists to consider. But I should be much surprised if it would be possible for the Irish, by any imposition of import duties or otherwise, to do our trade as much harm as the insecurity due to the present quarrel is causing it. Ireland is commercially dependent on us far more than we are on Ireland, and so would remain. The only point I recognize as a serious difficulty is that of the property held by Englishmen in Ireland. Engagements no doubt have been entered into by the Imperial Government toward the holders of Irish land and those who have invested money there on mortgage. This seems to me an imperial obligation, and if there is loss, imperial funds should, in my opinion, be held responsible. But I consider the danger of confiscation enormously exaggerated; and I do not conceive that an Irish more than any other Government would separate itself from that on which all Governments rely for strength—the interests of property. My best advice to Irish landlords would be that they should take their part in the general political movement of the country, and so retain their control over it. I believe that were they to do so, they would be well able to hold their own under Home Rule.

Let Ireland then have what she demands, self-government; she does not ask for separation from the Crown; and I am confident that neither in purse nor in political strength would England be any poorer. She would regain, on the contrary, her freedom of action, and relieve herself before the world of the stigma of a long oppression which has become a scandal, and a hindrance alike to her moral and material progress.

It will be observed that I pay little heed to the contention, now commonly raised, that the Irish people are under compulsion from their leaders when they demand Home Rule. This cry is always raised when nations begin to ask for anything unpalatable to their rulers; and my experience in Egypt and elsewhere has taught me to be profoundly sceptical of the argument that a people can be terrorized by their own chosen representatives, or by secret societies of their own founding to their own prejudice. A certain class there is, and a certain section of the inhabitants of Ireland, who see their interest in maintaining the Union on its present basis. But the immense mass of the Irish are enthusiastically against it. I know also too well how unscrupulously public opinion in England is worked up through the press, wherever material interests are involved, or supposed to be involved. The power of money is nowhere more apparent than in questions of this sort; and there is every probability that the English people will be deceived on the Irish as they have been on the Egyptian and Indian questions by those whose immediate financial interests lie in distorting the truth. Only, there will some day be a rude awakening. These are the cases that make one despair of popular government as compatible with empire.

WILFRID SCAWEN BLUNT.

A. I. TILLYARD, M.A. CAMB.

THE Home Rule question will before long have to be decided by the direct vote of the English people. On that vote will hang issues more tremendous than have hung on any previous exercise of the franchise. Woe, then, to our country if her electors have a wrong opinion or no opinion in this matter. But how are ordinary people to come to a conclusion in a matter that baffles statesmen and divides parties? We of the rank and file, if I may speak as one of them, need not pretend to have mastered all the sad facts of Ireland's history, to understand thoroughly the inner life and conflicting interests of its divided people, or to pronounce authoritatively on every detail of a Home Rule scheme; but only to be alive to certain great facts, which they who run may read.

In the first place, the Empire is dismembered already. It is the Disunited Kingdom of Great Britain and Ireland, and always has been. Separation itself could scarce make things worse. Ireland laughs when we have distress at home or disaster abroad. The greater Ireland in the United States and the Colonies acts in concert with the forces of disaffection at our gates. There is more union between us and our self-governing Colonies, there is more union between us and the separate people of the United States, than between us and Ireland. The problem is how to substitute moral union for force union, and so establish for the first time the unity of the Empire.

Moral union can only be brought about by legislating in accordance with the wishes of the Irish people. The Irish demand is for self-government—a demand that, uncomplicated by other issues, naturally appeals to every Liberal. Why should not the Irish govern themselves? Because the Irish people are not to be trusted. Every argument against Home Rule comes back to this. But distrust of the people is Toryism; trust in the people is Liberalism. Tangled as are the details of the Irish problem, never was there a simpler or a clearer case of principle. I for one elect to stand to my principles, and to trust the Irish people. Let us as a nation say to our Irish brethren: "Here are the destinies of Ireland for you to make or mar." Surely the answer will be: "We will make them, not mar them."

What does distrusting the Irish people imply? It implies that the leading men of Ireland, the home of the most passionate devotion to country, are ignorant of the very meaning of the word patriotism, that they would sacrifice everything at home to cupidity and religious intolerance, and everything abroad, to spite England. *Cras credam.* Our own experience ought to keep us from arguing what men will do when they are responsible, from what they do when they are irresponsible. It is a commonplace of politics that office makes Liberals turn Conservative, and Conservatives turn Liberal—so great is the difference between a responsible Government and an irresponsible Opposition. The case is much stronger with regard to the Nationalists. Make them responsible for the welfare of Ireland, and the tactics adopted to wring consent from an unwilling Government would be changed for efforts used to restore prosperity to a country impoverished by centuries of misgovernment and oppression, and torn by internal conflict. Human nature is the same on both sides of the

Irish Sea. Mistrust has brought out its worst characteristics; faith will bring out its best.

This argument does not apply to measures of half-trust. A half measure of local government would be dangerous. It would bring but a limited sense of responsibility, and leave national aspirations ungratified. Local institutions would be worked, not for their proper ends, but to obtain larger concessions. Tinkering legislation has been our bane long enough. We must trust the Irish people "not at all, or all in all."

Some are frightened at the threats of the Orange Party (who are a portion only of Irish Protestants), that they will bring about civil war rather than tolerate Home Rule. These threats were heard before, and came to nothing. An alternative policy has already been declared by some Orangemen. They will either fight or *leave the country*. The probabilities are, they will do neither. Liberals will hardly care to follow a policy toward Ireland dictated by the party whose watchword is the supremacy of the few over the many, and brute force to back it up. Yet between this policy of coercion and the policy of conciliation, pure and simple, there will be found to be no logical halting-place. England and Ireland are necessary to each other, and were designed by Nature to be friends. Paradoxical as it may appear, to loosen the present bonds in the spirit of confidence and goodwill, is to tie the sister isle fast to us for evermore.

A. I. TILLYARD.

J. O'CONNOR POWER.

I HAVE been for many years a consistent supporter of a federal union between Great Britain and Ireland, and during the eleven years that I sat in the House of Commons as the representative of an Irish county I never lost an opportunity of stating my views upon the subject. What I am now about to say will be only a brief summary of what I have already published by speech and writing.

One great advantage to be gained by Irish self-government is constantly overlooked. The Irish representatives sitting in Dublin would have to answer to the Irish people for the acts of their own Government. The Irish Government would have an Irish Opposition to encounter, and the disaffection which is now visited upon the British Cabinet would be directed by Irishmen against their native rulers. Make the Irish leaders responsible, and you take away at once one-half of their power with their own countrymen, and you deprive them at the same time, and in a still greater degree, of the power of annoying or injuring you.

The schemes for self-government in Ireland which have been proposed for our acceptance are of almost every form and variety known to civilized states. Not only have we different proposals from different sets of politicians, but we have different proposals from politicians in the same set. "Grattan's Parliament," "Ireland like Canada," "National Councils," "Grand Committees composed exclusively of Irish members," and other phrases, have been used to indicate a plan or promote a policy; but self-government on the basis of a federal union seems to me to be the only practicable scheme of the many which have been proposed. Under Grattan's Parliament there was no Irish Administration responsible to Irish opinion. The Irish Government consisted of the Viceroy and his secretary and their subordinates. They went into and out of office with the English Government, and were independent of any vote of the Irish Legislature. As for the Canadian example, it must be remembered that the only visible bond connecting Canada with Great Britain is the Governor-Generalship. Canada consents to accept her chief ruler from London, providing for him an establishment at Ottawa and a salary of 50,000 dollars a year. He acts on the advice of his Canadian Ministers, and in exchange for this slight acknowledgment of her dependence Canada enjoys the protection of the British arms. Of course, like the other colonies, she leaves to the Imperial Parliament all questions of foreign policy, but possesses commercial freedom and full power over her own tariffs and revenues, besides the power to raise militia and volunteers. If Ireland were as far away from England as Canada, the latter might well serve as a model for a new Irish Constitution; but as she is within four hours' sail of Holyhead, this solution of the Anglo-Irish problem will, I think, be dismissed as impracticable. The federal scheme was adopted at a Home Rule Conference held in Dublin in 1873, when Mr. Butt was the leader of the Irish party, and fifty-nine Irish members were returned to Parliament in the following year to support it. It has undergone one important modification since; whereas it was intended originally to restore the Irish House of Lords, it is now proposed to copy the United States model, and substitute an elective Senate for the Irish Second Chamber. If Ireland held a position similar to that of a State in the American Union, her internal affairs would be regulated by an Irish Parliament. Imperial affairs—everything relating to the colonies, the relations of the Empire with foreign States, the disposition of the naval and military forces, the levying of imperial taxes for imperial purposes, and the issues of peace and war—would be regulated, as at present, by the Imperial Parliament, in which Ireland would be represented when imperial affairs only were under consideration. Ireland had no representation in the Imperial Parliament prior to the Union, but the power she possessed of influencing British policy was of a much more dangerous character; for, having absolute control of her own finance, she had the power to withhold supplies in time of war. In a federal arrangement the prerogatives of the Crown would remain untouched; Great Britain and Ireland would each transact its own business in its own way; while for all imperial purposes the two countries would continue to be one imperial State. I do not believe that the relations between Austria and Hungary, or those between Norway and Sweden, are examples to be followed. They carry us farther in the direction of decentralization than is at all necessary for the purposes of self-government; I mean such self-government as is at all admissible—self-government which is compatible with the integrity of the United Kingdom. Among foreign nations the United States supplies the highest example of local self-government combined with imperial unity. There are thirty-eight Home Rule Parliaments for the thirty-eight States of the Union, and one Imperial Parliament at Washington, whose authority in all imperial affairs is unquestioned and unquestionable. Scarcely a single writer has dealt with the Irish question recently without making some reference to the American Union, and those who have written most strongly against any form of Home Rule in Ireland have referred to the determination with which the

North put down the rebellion of the South, and sacrificed everything for the Union, as an illustration of what England is prepared to do in order to preserve the union with Ireland. But there is some confusion of ideas and inconsistency of reasoning in this appeal to the conduct of the United States. The North put down the rebellion of the Southern States in 1865, as England did the Irish rebellion in 1798; but the North did not destroy the legislative independence of the Southern rebels, as England did that of the Irish ones; and if we are to imitate the North in her determination to maintain the Union, we must not be surprised if we are called upon to imitate her also in her recognition of States' rights and local freedom.

There is no necessity, however, to go outside the limits of the Empire for an example, whenever the state of public feeling in Ireland admits of this grave question being considered on its merits with a view to a final settlement. The Act of Confederation, combining the British North American provinces under the title of the Dominion of Canada, and the debates which took place in the Canadian Parliament, throw a good deal of light on the subject. The question—How are you to define what affairs are Irish and what are imperial? is here answered very clearly. The powers of the provincial Parliaments are strictly and clearly defined, as well as those of the Dominion Parliament at Ottawa, and no serious difficulty has arisen in the working of the system since it was established in 1867. Some of the oldest and most experienced politicians in Canada prophesied all manner of civil strife in the working of the Confederation Act, but their dismal forebodings have never come to pass. The strongest objection to a federal arrangement which I have seen stated is that it leaves the Irish representation in the Imperial Parliament as it is now, and that in imperial affairs, though not in English and Scotch affairs, the Irish members would still have the power of disturbing the proceedings of the Legislature and coercing the Government of the day. I maintain, on the contrary, that they would not have this power, and that if they had, they would have no sufficient motive for exercising it. The Irish members returned to the Imperial Parliament after the establishment of Home Rule would represent, not one party, but two—the Irish Government and the Irish Opposition. They would carry their differences with them to London, just as Republicans and Democrats from New York or California carry their differences to Washington. It is feared that they might combine to extort a further measure of independence for the Irish Parliament; but if such a thing were attempted, it should be treated as a breach of faith and of the understanding on which alone any scheme of Home Rule could be sanctioned, and, so treated, it would be easily disposed of.

To prevent the Imperial Parliament from being made an arena of conflict on the interpretation of the limits of its own powers and those of the local Parliament, I would amalgamate the Privy Councils of the United Kingdom, and erect them into a Supreme Court of Appeal for the settlement of all disputed questions arising between the local and imperial authority. The English Privy Council performs these functions at present in respect of provincial and dominion authority in Canada. The powers of such a court would, I am convinced, be very rarely invoked or exercised, and they would be limited strictly to the duty of judicial interpretation. It would have no power to interfere in any way with Irish legislation within its own proper limits, such as the English Privy Council had in the last century; and it would be above the control and beyond the influence of the Government of the day. Where, then, would be the motive for Irish obstruction in the Imperial Parliament? If the

Irish members made any demand for grants of imperial money, they would be told plainly that they must rely on their own resources, of which they would have absolute control, subject to the payment of Ireland's quota to imperial expenditure. In the course of time the Irish members would divide themselves into Liberals and Conservatives, like the English and Scotch members, and so contribute according to their party predilections to the regular and orderly government of a united empire. It may be taken for granted that if the Privy Council were entrusted with the duties here assigned to it, it would be reconstituted in such a way as to admit within its ranks the best legal talent and the highest political ability in the three kingdoms. If it be suggested that Ireland would not be satisfied with such a court of appeal because her Privy Councillors would necessarily be in a minority as compared with those of Great Britain, it must be answered that the integrity of the United Kingdom must at all hazards be preserved, and that if Ireland is to enjoy legislative independence within the Empire she must submit to effective imperial control.

I look upon it as an essential condition of any settlement of the Irish national question, that whatever is done should be the result of open and avowed agreement between the representatives of Great Britain on the one hand and those of Ireland on the other. Better not to touch the question at all unless it can be dealt with finally. Whatever is cheerfully conceded on one side should be as cheerfully accepted on the other—not as an instalment, but as a settlement. Then, next to the paramount necessity for preserving the unity of the Empire is the indispensable condition that the minority shall, while justly deprived of the power of ruling the majority, have the fullest guarantees against persecution or oppression; and the powers to be conferred on an Irish Legislature must be consistent with the primary conditions of civilized society in this age, the enforcement of law and order, the security of property, and the maintenance of religious liberty. The existing system, it must be admitted, fails to give the minority the protection which they demand, because in the nature of things it is impossible. If they had not accustomed themselves to rely on British bayonets they would have made a better use of their own resources; if they had not been pampered in ascendency they would have long since learnt how to live on terms of equality with the rest of their fellow-countrymen; if they had not grossly neglected the duties of property, they would not now be engaged in a desperate struggle to maintain its rights; and if even now they had wit enough to perceive and sense enough to embrace a great opportunity, they might obtain better terms from their own countrymen than the Imperial Parliament can secure for them. The minority in Ireland can do far more for themselves when thrown on their own resources than any exterior power can do for them. Home Rule or no Home Rule, the Imperial Parliament should never surrender the right, in the last resort, to put down disorder and prevent civil war. It should retain the power, which the United States Government has, of sending the military forces of the Central Government into any State where the local forces are unable or unwilling to preserve order. And if the expenses of the expedition were levied on the area of the disturbance, it would be a just penalty for the violation of the public peace. But the minority should not be looking perpetually to the British Government for help; it should rely on its own courage and resolution, and not absolutely despise those arts of conciliation which minorities in every country have to exercise in order to live in harmony with those around them. If the Irish police should be confined to those purely civil duties which they discharge in England and Scotland, I see no danger in leaving the control of them in Irish hands. Under any system of representative county government, such as we expect to see established before long, the police in every part of the United Kingdom will come under the control of the new county authorities, and nothing better could happen in Ireland than that the Royal Irish Constabulary should cease to be a national force, and become a purely local force, for local purposes, under local management and control. By reserving the organization of the militia and volunteers, as well as the army and navy, to imperial authority, the Irish Government would have nothing whatever to do with an armed force, and would be deprived of the means of physical resistance to the supreme authority of the Imperial Parliament, should, unhappily, any conflict arise between them. As to the detection of crime, I cannot doubt that the instinct of self-preservation alone would be sufficient to induce the local authorities in Irish counties to take adequate measures to that end; and I am convinced that their sense of responsibility would change entirely their present attitude of indifference into one of active sympathy with all the processes of the criminal law. No one proposes, as far as I know, to interfere with or remove the present occupants of the Bench, either at Petty Sessions or Quarter Sessions, or in the Superior Courts; and the judicial administration of the law would therefore remain for many years in the hands of those to whom it is now entrusted.

The struggle for the possession of the soil in Ireland is as old as the English occupation, and in its present aspect it is one of the great difficulties in the way of a satisfactory solution of the national question. The Land Act of 1881 is one of the greatest measures of justice ever placed upon any statute-book, and it will remain for all time a noble monument of the statesmanship of Mr. Gladstone, and of his unrivalled power as a legislator. That it has not solved all the difficulties of Irish land tenure is a testimony to the desperate character of the evils which it was designed to remove, and shows that, independently of agrarian agitation, there are economic causes at work which make it impossible that any solution should be final which does not combine ownership with occupation. Landlordism has broken down utterly and irretrievably in Ireland, and it is on the decline in every part of the United Kingdom. The pressure of economic forces is diminishing the power of landlordism in Great Britain, as the pressure of political forces has diminished it in Ireland; and when the British taxpayer is invited to buy out the Irish landlord, he may think twice before consenting to do anything of the kind. The Irish landlord is now very anxious to sell, as nobody in Ireland wants to buy. He appeals to England, and hopes to extract from her sympathy or necessity that which, on the ground of justice alone, he has no right to demand. If, however, it be apprehended that under Home Rule the tenants would refuse to pay their rents, and combine to confiscate the property of their landlords, the latter have a right to insist on guarantees from the Irish Government against such injustice; and as the British Government is not likely to assume the burden of ownership itself, even for a limited time, I know of no more equitable and effective arrangement than that which would make the Irish Government responsible for the fulfilment of contracts, by enabling the landlord, in every case where judicial rents were not paid, to sell his interest to that Government, on terms to be determined by the Land Commission or one of the superior courts of justice. The influence of the Irish Government would then be exercised on the side of contracts, lest it should be called upon to take the place of the landlord.

As to religious liberty, I have no apprehension that it would be endangered by the concession of self-government to Ireland. Religious persecution, of which Irish Catholics have had their share, is a powerful teacher of the virtue of religious toleration, and I have no doubt that the Protestant minority in Ireland would be as safe under Home Rule as the Catholic minority is in England under the Imperial Parliament. Certainly it would have a much larger proportionate representation in the Irish Parliament than the Catholics of Great Britain have at Westminster. The Irish Catholic constituencies have in a great many cases returned Catholics to represent them, and in my experience of Irish elections I have never known a single instance in a Catholic constituency where a candidate otherwise acceptable was opposed on the ground of his religious belief. The time has gone by, it is to be hoped, on both sides of the Channel, when considerations of this kind could influence the choice of a representative to serve in the Legislature, where members of all classes and creeds meet on a footing of equality, and where, according to the theory of our constitution, each is a representative not merely for his own constituency, but for the nation at large. O'Connell used to say that he was willing to take his theology from Rome, but not his politics. Besides, there exists among the Catholic laity a feeling which resents anything in the shape of clerical dictation in matters political; and in an Irish Parliament this feeling would assert itself on the slightest provocation. Any proposal to impose disabilities on the Protestant minority would, I am convinced, be voted down by a large majority of the Catholic members. The world has grown too wise for bigotry and intolerance; and the persecution of opinion is no longer regarded as a means of conversion, but as one of the surest agencies to render conversion impossible. The Imperial Parliament will reserve to itself, as the United States Congress at Washington does, the duty of guarding freedom of conscience. No State of the American Union may pass any law depriving any citizen of the United States of his civil rights on account of his religion. Our legislation for the last three-quarters of a century has been largely occupied in removing privileges and distinctions set up in a less enlightened age for the benefit of particular classes and creeds, and it is not tolerable, nor even conceivable, that any part of the United Kingdom should ever again be allowed to revert to the expedients which have been thus discredited and repudiated.

It is said that federalism is a system devised for securing cohesion among States, and that it is not applicable where your object is decentralization; but this argument cuts both ways, for it shows that federalism was applicable at the time of the Union, and if a blunder was committed then in not adopting it—as can, I think, easily be shown—there is no good reason why that blunder should not be repaired. If the Act of 1800 had effected a real and solid union, the case would be very different from what it is; but, as a matter of fact, the problem with which Pitt had to deal still remains to be solved. It cannot be denied that the powers exercised by Grattan's Parliament were incompatible with imperial authority, but what was needed was, not the destruction of the Parliament, but the modification of its powers. Federalism combines all the advantages of union and excludes all the dangers of separation, while at the same time it makes Irish freedom secure, and maintains the supreme authority of the Imperial Parliament.

J. O'CONNOR POWER.

REV. T. J. LAWRENCE,

OF DOWNING COLLEGE, CAMBRIDGE; VICAR OF LUDLOW.

A LARGE section of the British public is suffering from a bad attack of political hysterics. Sturdy Liberals are forgetting the first principles of Liberalism; great authors are shrieking against the proposals they themselves advocated in wiser and soberer moments; learned judges are leaving the calm of the bench and descending into the political arena as gladiators of the most pugnacious type; respectable peers are positively foaming at the mouth with vituperative rage; Clubdom is up in arms; and the *Times*, in full accoutrement of feathers, paint, and tomahawk, has gone on the war path,—a fearful and wonderful spectacle to behold. What is it all about? Separation, dismemberment of the Empire, paltering with treason, surrender to dynamite, mad and wicked ambition—all these and a host of similar cries are heard amid the turmoil. No two persons agree as to the exact nature of the terrible evil with which we are threatened, but all assert that it is something very dreadful indeed. And the remedy is as mysterious as the disease. It must of course be drastic. We are just now in the mood for heroics. Something short, sharp, and decisive is wanted. If we only hit hard enough, all will be well. It is true we have not yet settled who we are to hit, or where our blow is to be planted, or with what sort of weapon it is to be inflicted. But these are unimportant details. The great thing is to make somebody feel. That done, the unknown disease of the body politic will immediately be cured, and we shall go on our majestic way rejoicing in having given to the world a new proof of the vast wisdom which we invariably show in managing our Irish affairs. Such at least is the opinion of the profound political thinkers who spend most of their time lounging in the clubs of Pall Mall, and the omniscient gentlemen who write the editorials of the London Press. What the new democracy thinks is not so evident. I shall be very much surprised if it should turn out that the workers in field and forge and factory share the panic of their self-appointed instructors.

Let us try to look calmly at the situation in Ireland, without being swayed in one direction by unmanly panic, or in the other by foolish optimism. The first thing to notice is that the problem which confronts us, terribly complicated though it be, is less dark and confused than it was a short time ago. We now know what Ireland really wants. For the first time in history the voice of the Irish people has been heard speaking in a perfectly unmistakable and at the same time perfectly lawful and constitutional manner. Household suffrage has made the country articulate. Previously we knew what were the wishes of selected classes; now we know what the whole nation desires. And whereas in former days the representatives of Irish constituencies were of all shades of political opinion, from Orange Tories to Republican Separatists, and no one shade had any marked preponderance; now there are but two parties among them, and of these one is so much stronger than the other that it may be considered for all practical purposes as the people of Ireland. We may dismiss with the contempt they deserve the ingenious attempts that have been made to prove that, though 85 Irish members out of 103 are followers of Mr. Parnell, yet in reality he has but a bare majority of the Irish people at his back. The thousands upon thousands of so-called loyalists, who could not muster sufficient courage to record a secret vote in defence of all they hold dear, are as purely imaginary as Falstaff's men in buckram. Nor is the theory that a few daring spirits terrorized their neighbours into voting as one man for Home Rule candidates worthy of much consideration. Such explanations of opposition are the commonplaces of tyranny. Either foreign emissaries or domestic traitors have invariably misled a too-confiding people, who, if only they were left to themselves, would live in happiness under a paternal rule. So reasoned the Sultan when Bulgaria revolted in 1876. So reasoned the Czar when Poland rose in 1863. So reasoned Charles I. when the English people refused to pay his unconstitutional exactions. And so reason our would-be terrorists of to-day. We have heard it all before not so very long ago, and believed it too, till we learned by sad experience how false it was. In 1881 Mr. Forster told us that power to lock up the "village ruffians," who were at the bottom of all outrages, would enable him to rule Ireland in peace. He got the power; and he used it till the prisons overflowed with his suspects. And the result was a general revolt against all law and order on the part of the population that was supposed to be so docile, while a very considerable proportion of the men who were then sent to gaol have been elected by their neighbours to represent them in the present Parliament. Turn and twist the matter as we may, there is no escape from the fact that we are confronted by a demand for Home Rule from three-quarters of the Irish people, including half the population of Ulster.

It is a gain to know what Ireland wants; and instead of trying all sorts of futile devices to persuade ourselves that she does not mean what she says, it will be wise to sit down calmly and see if we cannot meet her wishes in such a way as to content her, without giving up anything that we hold essential to the security of the Empire. Surely we have had enough of blunt refusals, followed first by stern coercion and then by humiliating concessions. To go back no further than the present century, the long denial of the full rights of citizenship to Roman Catholics was followed by the surrender of 1829, which was forced from the Tory Government of the day in order to avoid civil war. And again, the refusal to concede anything to the Tenant Right movement of 1850 led to the Land Acts of 1870 and 1881. We are told that Home Rule means separation and dismemberment of the Empire. If it does, I make bold to say that England will never grant it; but a very little knowledge of the political constitutions of civilized states is sufficient to show that wide rights of local and even national self-government are quite compatible with imperial unity. Our glib instructors, whose indignant patriotism fills the correspondence columns of the *Times* with burning denunciations of the Home Rule project, are wonderfully ignorant of a whole class of important facts which it behoves them to study carefully at the present juncture. Austria is a bundle of nationalities, all of whom have assemblies of their own to manage their local affairs. Germany is a great confederation. Even Russia allows Finland to retain its ancient Parliament. The world bristles with instances of subordinate and local councils, ranging in power and attributes from parochial vestries to national Parliaments. Surely somewhere along the extended line can be found an assembly fitted to be the type of a Home Rule Parliament in Dublin. It is not so very long ago since Lord Salisbury in his Newport speech directed our attention to the relations between Austria and Hungary. Our "men of light and leading" are far more likely to find a solution of the Irish difficulty in the study of the constitutional expedients by which similar difficulties have been overcome elsewhere, than by shrieking themselves hoarse with impotent denunciations of Mr. Parnell and his followers. The statesmen of England are not so far inferior to those of other countries as to be baffled by problems which have been solved with more or less completeness by some of the leading nations of the world. Our own kindred beyond the Atlantic have reconciled complete local self-government with absolute external unity. Taking as the basis of negotation the position of a State in the American Union, we might be able to come to an agreement with the Irish leaders which would satisfy the reasonable aspirations of Ireland, while it retained unimpaired imperial sovereignty in imperial affairs.

But it will be said that in Ireland the political problem is only one branch of the difficulty. An agrarian revolution is in full swing, and we cannot surrender the landlords to be dealt with as may seem good to an Irish Parliament. Undoubtedly there is much force in this contention. Though as a class the Irish landowners are deserving of very little sympathy, yet seeing that England has in times gone by placed them and maintained them in the country as a bulwark of her own rule, it would be dishonourable in her now to leave them to the tender mercies of a nation demoralized by their oppressions, and only too ready to put in practice the lessons of dishonesty in agrarian matters which were taught by English law during the time it allowed the owners of the soil to confiscate the improvements of their tenants. But the scheme of expropriation recently made public by Mr. Giffen solves this difficulty in the most effective manner, while at the same time it enlists on the side of honesty the very men whose influence is now too often used in favour of a very loose interpretation of the Eighth Commandment. If Great Britain bought out the landlords at a reasonable price, and handed over the rent of the land to the new local Irish government in lieu of those expenses of administration which she now bears, we may be perfectly certain Mr. Parnell and his lieutenants would find means to get in the revenue thus assigned to them, and that the Irish peasants would cheerfully pay to rulers of their own choice a land tax which will be spent on objects they approve, especially as the tax is to be considerably less than their present rent. And if the worst comes to the worst, and John Bull loses some of his cash in the process of pacifying Ireland, he must be content to suffer in pocket for his past misdeeds. A pecuniary loss which closes the era of repression and hatred will in reality be great gain.

If once the land question is satisfactorily settled, I believe that the pacification of Ireland under some scheme of Home Rule will not be a task of insuperable difficulty. We need not take seriously the threats of the so-called loyalists, who show their loyalty by threatening to kick the Queen's crown into the Boyne, and line with rifles every ditch in Ulster, if their position of ascendency is touched. The same wild words were spoken when the Disestablishment of the Irish Church was mooted, but the fire-eaters never ventured upon action. They are contemptible in numbers and intelligence; and assuredly the sturdy common-sense of Irish Protestantism would never countenance a policy of rebellion. Mr. Parnell himself is a Protestant, as Swift and Grattan and Plunkett were before him. If Protestants cordially accept the new order of things, they will have nothing to fear. The old monopoly of office and emolument will indeed disappear; but in its stead will arise an ascendency based upon culture, capacity, and popular sympathy, and in all these, Protestants need be at no disadvantage compared with their Roman Catholic fellow-citizens.

The only alternative to Home Rule is coercion of the sternest kind. The present state of things is admitted on all hands to be intolerable. Somehow or other we must make the law obeyed, and there are only two ways of attaining so desirable an end. England, being far more powerful than Ireland, can drive, drill, dragoon, and shoot the Irish people, till they submit to whatever laws she chooses to impose upon them. Only she must continue the process from year to year, and from generation to generation. She must be hard and ruthless, not by fits and starts, but always and on every occasion. She must abolish the farce of parliamentary representation, and tell the Irish people that for the future she intends to rule them without regard to their wishes. She must find a Strafford or a Cromwell, and set him over them with dictatorial power. His behests must be law, and an irresistible force must be at his disposal to compel obedience to them.

This is one alternative. The other is to enlist the people on the side of order by conceding to them a Government which they approve, administered by leaders of their own choice. Half-measures are ridiculous and impossible. What, for instance, would come of giving county government, except that there would soon be thirty-two local assemblies in Ireland, all, or nearly all, devoted to Mr. Parnell, and determined to make decent administration impossible till Home Rule was granted?

The people of England will not be content for long to rule Ireland by the sword. In a fit of irritation and panic they may consent to try the experiment; but better feelings will soon arise, and one party or the other will find its advantage in proposing concession. And if we are to concede, why should we not do so at once, without wasting the time and energy of Parliament on a new Coercion Bill, and laying up a fresh store of hatred against England in the breasts of the Irish people ? Statesmen must decide whether Home Rule is to be granted by the present Parliament. Meanwhile it may not be amiss to recall, and apply to the present crisis, the warning addressed by Brougham to the House of Lords on the night when it threw out Earl Grey's Reform Bill:—" As sure as man is mortal and to err is human, justice deferred enhances the price at which you must purchase safety and peace ; nor can you expect to gather in another crop than they did who went before you, if you persist in their utterly abominable husbandry of sowing injustice and reaping rebellion."

T. J. LAWRENCE.

T. P. O'CONNOR, M.P.

WE impeach the Act of Union as the cause of enormous evil to England and to Ireland; and we demand its repeal or its modification.

First, we demand it because our experience of a partially independent Parliament was encouraging, and our experience of a united Parliament is disastrous. The Parliament of the ante-Union days was most defective. The members of but one creed, and that the creed of the smallest numbers, were admissible within its walls. The House of Lords was hopelessly and almost entirely servile and corrupt; and of the three hundred members of the House of Commons above two hundred were returned by individuals, from forty to fifty were returned by ten persons; several of the boroughs had no resident at all; two-thirds of the entire number were returned by less than one hundred persons; and one hundred had places or pensions.

Yet that body advanced, according to the confession of one of its destroyers—Fitz-Gibbon, Lord Clare—the material prosperity of Ireland with extraordinary rapidity. Created in the narrowest spirit of bigotry, it showed a most liberal spirit; its destruction marked an enormous aggravation in the sectarian spirit of Ireland. In 1778 the purely Protestant Parliament restored Catholics to the equal enjoyment of all property they held, and enabled them to acquire long terms for years in lands. In 1782 the Protestant Parliament restored to the Catholics the right to acquire freehold property; in 1792 and 1793 the learned professions were opened to a certain extent to Catholics ; in 1793 the elective franchise was restored to the Catholics by the Protestant Parliament ;* and finally with regard to the old Irish Parliament its destruction was admittedly obtained by means as foul as any recorded in English history.

The demand for the restoration of our Parliament, among other things, is denounced as a demand involving a revolutionary innovation. But, as everybody knows, there was an Irish Parliament for centuries, and its destruction took place but eighty-five years ago. To demand a return to a state of relations that existed for centuries, and that only ceased to exist less than a century ago, cannot be called, except by an abuse of terms, a demand for a revolutionary innovation. Then our methods are described as revolutionary. But we make the demand in the name of 85 representatives out of an entire representation of 103 members. We make it in the Imperial Parliament. It would be hard to put forward a demand in a form more constitutional.

How an Englishman, who believes in countries being governed in accordance with the wishes of their peoples, can oppose the claim for Home Rule thus put forward by the Irish people, is very hard to understand.

But is the demand wise or well-founded? We have had eighty-five years' experience of the Act of Union. From almost the hour of its birth—more, from the hour of its contemplation—the Act of Union created disloyalty in Ireland and discomfort in England. Pitt looked forward to the Union many years before it was proposed. "The standing object," writes Lecky, "of his later Irish policy was to corrupt and to degrade, in order that he might ultimately de-

* O'Connell, quoted by J. G. S. MacNeill : "The Irish Parliament," pp. 96-5.

stroy, the Legislature of the country."* It was Pitt's refusal of parliamentary reform that transformed the United Irishmen from loyal reformers into revolutionaries; † and it was Pitt's recall of Lord Fitzwilliam, with the same purpose of carrying the Union, that brought about the rebellion of '98. The united Parliament had scarcely begun to sit when it had to pass Coercion Acts for Ireland. Coercion is the clumsy and fatal instrument by which Governments seek to perpetuate themselves over unwilling subjects. The Act of Union made British rule hateful in Ireland. Coercion has, therefore, been necessary to make British rule possible; and the united Parliament has been kept pretty busy with Coercion. In the eighty-five years which have elapsed since the Union the Imperial Parliament has passed eighty-our Coercion Acts.

The cause of religious as well as civil liberty went back with the destruction of the Irish Parliament. In 1823 Lord Nugent sought to extend to English Catholics the voting privilege conferred by the Irish Protestant Parliament on Irish Catholics. The measure miscarried in the Lords, and, though frequently brought into Parliament, did not become law. It was not until 1829 that English Catholics got the vote. In 1794 Lord Fitzwilliam was sent to Ireland to carry Catholic Emancipation; he was able to assure the King of "the universal approbation with which the emancipation of the Catholics was viewed on the part of his Protestant subjects." ‡ He wrote to Lord Carlisle that "not one Protestant corporation—scarcely one individual—had come forward to deprecate and oppose the indulgence claimed by the higher order of Catholics." § Grattan obtained, immediately after, leave to bring in an

---

* " Leaders of Public Opinion in Ireland," p. 146.
† Ibid. p. 140.   ‡ Ibid. p. 147.   § Ibid. p. 144.

Emancipation Bill, with but three dissentients; and "few facts," writes Lecky, "in Irish history are more certain than that the Irish Parliament would have carried Emancipation if Lord Fitzwilliam had remained in power."* Lecky thus fixes the probable date of Emancipation as 1795—thirty-four years before it was obtained from the United Parliament. "But for the Union," says an even higher authority, "full and complete Emancipation would have been carried before 1803." †

In the one great industry of the Irish people the Union was above all things destructive. Everybody now knows the dread and full meaning of the land question in the economy of Irish life. As it has been put, the possession of land means the difference between existence and starvation. If the Irish Parliament had remained in existence, it is easy to see that the freedom of the land would have followed almost as rapidly as the freedom of the Church. The Parliament that gave the Irish Catholics votes, that was largely favourable to parliamentary reform, and that was ready to admit Catholic members, would have been ready, and indeed would have been necessarily compelled, to carry out a land policy in accordance with the wishes and the interests of the masses of the people. It is probable that half a century ago, if the Irish Parliament had not been destroyed, a Bill would have been passed giving the tenants rights as great as they had to wait for until the days of the Land League and the Act of Mr. Gladstone in 1881.

If Englishmen could be got to realize all this means, they would passionately sympathize with, instead of bitterly opposing, the Irish demand for a native Parliament.

* " Leaders of Public Opinion in Ireland," p. 151.
† O'Connell, quoted by MacNeill Swift, "Irish Parliament," &c., p. 95.

For what does it mean ? It means that if the Irish Parliament had lasted, Ireland would have been saved three famines, a million and half of deaths by hunger, the exile of at least three millions of her people, three abortive rebellions, and many cycles of horrible cruelty by landlords and horrible crime by tenants. For a bad land system is at the bottom of all the evils of Ireland. The right to raise the rent, to confiscate improvements, to evict, were the things which made famine inevitable ; through famine, produced plague, wholesale death, universal emigration ; and those rights of the landlords the Imperial Parliament not only did nothing to check, but did much to increase and aggravate.

For the destruction of the Irish Parliament was followed by the deterioration of all nobility of spirit among the landlords, as among large sections of the Protestant population. Within a short period after the passage of the Act of Union, a whole eviction code had been manufactured under the sinister guidance of the late Sir Robert Peel ; and it was this code that, after the disfranchisement of the forty-shilling freeholder in 1829, enabled the landlords to begin that system of wholesale clearances which has laid waste so many parts of Ireland, has impoverished her towns and crowded her workhouses, and created the Ribbon Lodges and the other assassination leagues among the peasantry. It was the eviction code, again, that prepared the country for the dread famine of 1846 to 1849, and for all the horrors of that terrible epoch ; and it was thus that a population which in 1845 had reached to nearly nine millions of people had in 1851 been reduced to about six and a half.

If we look to the consequences to England, we find the Act of Union quite as disastrous. At the moment when the Act was under discussion in the Parliament House in College Green, the approaches were guarded by large masses of soldiers ready to put down any overt signs of discontent in blood. Ever since that moment England has been compelled to keep garrisons in Ireland to suppress any manifestations of popular discontent, and periodically to put down desperate though abortive attempts to remove intolerable wrongs by armed rebellion.

Within the shores of Ireland, then, the Act of Union has manufactured a large mass of disaffection—sometimes silent and sullen, and sometimes menacing and armed; and has rendered necessary a vast amount of expenditure, such as would be deemed intolerable in the case of any other dependency. The Act of Union, in addition, has compelled England to support in Ireland a huge force of constabulary —police only in name—drilled, armed, highly paid, thirteen thousand in number, and to all intents and purposes a portion of the armed garrison of the country. It is calculated that at the present moment the imperial expenses in Ireland are four millions and a half. So much of these four millions and a half as are paid by England and Scotland represent the fine which English and Scotch taxpayers have to pay for the luxury of governing Ireland against the will of her own people. Abroad, the Act of Union has created for England enemies even more fierce, and in some respects more dangerous, than the enemies she has left in Ireland. In America and in many of the British colonies there are Irishmen whose first knowledge of the law made by the Imperial and United Parliament came when, as shivering children, they saw their cursing fathers and weeping mothers driven out of their homes by landlords assisted by the representatives of English law and by the representatives of English force; and the late Professor Cairnes—a staunch Unionist and a scientific economist—declared that if he had passed along the road to the emigrant ship from a ruined home, as so many Irish exiles did, his feelings would have been those of bitter hate for the country and the laws that permitted such things. To English law, then, the Irish exiles in every part of the world bear bitter hate; there are few parts of the world to which large masses of the Irish people have not emigrated; and it is therefore one of the effects of the Act of Union to have girdled the world with enemies of English power and English rule.

Finally, these various things have made the Ireland of to-day one of the poorest, one of the most disturbed, and perhaps the saddest country in the civilized world. The Imperial Parliament has to be stirred to justice by fierce agitation; the still unnatural relations between the landlords and the tenants are the source of constant collisions and disturbance; capital flies from a country without security and without rest; the spirit of enterprise is dead in a land without the vivifying spirit of liberty; the towns are in a state of daily increasing decay; in the fields more acres are yearly drifting back into the desolate and untilled heath; the hæmorrhage of emigration goes on; the population is reduced to a little over one-half of what it once was; the people who go are the young and the strong—the people who remain are the old and the weak; the struggle for existence becomes every year more desperate; and the marriage-rate of Ireland is lower than that of almost any country in Europe.

Here, then, we have a country presenting as many of the morbid conditions of national life as could well exist. And how, on the other hand, is it with England? The life and heart and soul of the British Empire is in the House of Commons, and the House of Commons has ceased to be the pride and glory and guardian of the Empire. The former freedom of debate has been curtailed; new rules are constantly spoken of; the cumbrous machine is breaking down under its own weight; the smallest reform has to wait for years; and the temper of all parties has deteriorated. In that assembly, too, there is now an element which threatens to be omnipotent, which has less care for the Empire at large than for the welfare of Ireland, and which discusses and decides on almost every question, not from the Imperial but from the Irish standpoint. When debates take place on Imperial concerns it is the Irish vote that turns the scale in the division lobbies; but the Irish vote is dictated, not so much by considerations for the welfare of the Empire, as by regard for the welfare of Ireland. Parliament lies at the mercy of the representatives of one country in the whole Empire, and through these representatives Ministries can be upset, parties confused, the issues of the general elections and the votes of British electors nullified; in short, the Act of Union has ruined Ireland, and threatens the ruin of England through the ruin of her representative institutions.

One final element of derangement was added in the last election to the already full cauldron of anarchy and confusion. In England, the Irishmen driven by the Act of Union from Ireland have organized themselves into a great electoral force, turning, according to Mr. Trevelyan, no less than forty seats, and possibly destined to be able to decide whether England shall have a Conservative or a Liberal Administration; and this new force, like the Irish party in Parliament, while deciding English and Imperial struggles, will act with regard not to the interests of the Empire at large, but rather to the welfare of Ireland.

This is assuredly a sufficiently grave indictment against any one piece of legislation; and there are few impartial persons that will be bold enough to deny its accuracy. In any case, even those who contend that the Act of Union has led to the prosperity of Ireland and the strengthening of the Empire—and they will be sufficiently bold who will so contend—even those do not deny that the present state of things is intolerable, and cannot be allowed to continue. All parties having then arrived at the conclusion that something must be done, we come to the great question, What is to be done? Practically, opinion is pretty unanimous among men who think out policies, that there are but two alternatives—without any halfway house, without any possibility of compromise between. The two alternatives are the coercion of Ireland and the maintenance of the Union by the sword; or the repeal of the Union and the government of Ireland by Irishmen.

Though there be no possibility of compromise, there are not wanting po liticians who talk about it. Mr. Chamberlain has some plan of County Boards, ending in a National Council, which either may mean a vestry, in which case it is too little; or a Parliament, in which case it had better be called by the name as well as have the power of a Parliament. Then there is a good deal of pointless and stupid talk about the destruction of Dublin Castle. Dublin Castle is an inconvenient metonym. It may mean either the centralization of all authority and administration in the Lord Lieutenant; or it may mean the offices of a large number of the departments of the country. In the one case its abolition has some, though not much, intelligibility, for decentralization without a Legislature is impossible; in the latter case it is of course sheer nonsense, as many of the offices at present in Dublin Castle would have to be maintained under any system of Government. There are various other schemes; such as the representation of Ireland by a Minister, and the abolition of the Viceroyalty. A moment's reflection would show the utter futility of such a proposal. A Minister in the House of Commons implies the presence there also of the eighty-five Irish representatives; these eighty-five representatives are just as much opposed to the proposed, as to the present system, and the position of a Minister for Ireland, with eighty-five Irish representatives in constant and fierce hostility to him, is, of course, impossible. Then some people speak of a body in Dublin with some power over Railway and Water Bills. This, again, supposes the presence at Westminster of Irish members; and it can easily be supposed how workable would be a body in Dublin which had eighty-five representatives to attack the Minister for Ireland, and to use their voices in frequent discussion and their votes in critical divisions for enlarging the powers of this body. Assuredly every Englishman of sense would prefer that if an Irish Parliament is to be arrived at ultimately, the sooner the journey is travelled and at an end the better for his peace of mind. Then there are those who talk of a good County Bill as a settlement of the question. The reform of the scandalous and wicked Grand Jury system is of course one of the great necessities of Irish reform; but in what way will that get rid of the demand for Home Rule? The so-called Loyalist party in Ireland have already stated their views of such a scheme, and their declaration is, that reform of county government, instead of diminishing, will augment the strength of the party seeking legislative independence.

All these schemes of timid or illogical or shallow statesmanship may then be dismissed, and we are left to the two alternatives of government by the sword or government by consent.

But government by the sword, however easy to talk about in irresponsible newspaper articles, is impossible. It is certainly impossible for any length of time. There are always these eighty-five men, and the experience of Mr. Forster, when he had not half that number to deal with, will show how impossible it is to maintain a régime of coercion under the fierce and constant light of parliamentary interrogation and debate. Of course there is the power of disfranchising Ireland and expelling the eighty-five representatives; but every politician of note has denounced such an idea, from Lord Randolph Churchill downwards. The truth is, England cannot coerce. Proceeding to destroy the liberties of a nation like Ireland, she is in the position of Hamlet in the closet, denouncing his mother:

> " Do not look upon me," he says to his father's ghost,
> " Lest with this piteous action you convert
> My stern effects: then, what I have to do
> Will want true colour; tears, perchance, for blood."

What England has to do in suppressing liberty in Ireland will, ultimately at least, "want true colour." In stabbing at liberty, England is stabbing at the mother of her own prosperity, her own greatness, the largeness of her own place in the history of the world. When Mr. Gladstone was forecasting, in April 1882, the release of Mr. Parnell, he had to confess that coercion had broken down, because coercion was repugnant to the institutions of his country. Surely all experience must show this to be an inevitable fact of English political and party life—inevitable from both the good and the evil in this life. The hysterical demands of unpractical littérateurs, or judges speaking in national politics with the black cap suitable to the sentencing of a hapless wretch to violent death, may be left to shriek for more consistency and more brutality in coercion. Trained politicians ought to know that they might as well bay out their throats in calls for the moon. We saw two strong men practise coercion in Ireland within the last five years: Mr. Forster was thrown over by the Liberals, Lord Spencer was thrown over by the Tories; and so it will be with every Minister who makes himself the unhappy instrument of the fierce but brief passion of brutality that periodically passes over England in her dealings with Ireland.

To concession, then, it will ultimately come. There may be a dreary and perhaps even a terrible interval—with the frenzy of unbridled power on the one side, and the frenzy of despair on the other. Every true well-wisher of England or of Ireland, every humane man, every prudent and sensible statesman, ought to exhaust every effort rather than that the immediate future should be made so dark for either England or Ireland; and the responsibility of those who may have any share in bringing about such a state of relations between the two races, will be as great and terrible and shameful as almost that of any creator of causeless and foolish conflict in history. But the end, sooner or later, is sure. Irish history, as Sir Charles Gavan Duffy remarks, has, rightly examined, the consistency and unity of an epic. Throughout all the many centuries of connection between the two countries the aspiration for self-government runs— often timid and weak and sometimes even apparently dead, but there, all the same and all the time. And this great idea has features as astonishing as its duration. The present Irish movement marks not merely the unity of a nation, but also the unity of a race, and of a race scattered over many countries of the world, separated by daily life, by interests, by oceans, and by continents, from the cradle-land of the Irish race. If we turn to England, on the other hand, we find the idea of dominance growing weaker with every advancing year. Coercion is no longer applied to Ireland with a light heart, but with shamefacedness; the dealings of England with Ireland in the past are mentioned with an apology, and the differences between most intelligent and temperate Englishmen and intelligent and temperate Irishmen, as to the future relations between the two countries, are differences of degree rather than of principle. It is an unequal contest between England and Ireland, and Irish self-government is the assured victor.

The important question is, what form the new legislative

relations between the two countries should take. Many plans have been suggested: I have neither the right nor the desire to advance anything more than suggestions. Two fundamental principles should, I think, govern the whole settlement.

First, the Irish Parliament should be supreme within the shores of Ireland, and in dealing with purely Irish affairs; and secondly, the Empire is entitled to take due precautions against attacks upon its safety.

Ireland should be supreme within the shores of Ireland. This is a demand from which Irishmen should not recede; for it is the only settlement that is workable. Of course this implies the control of the police by the Irish Administration. The hubbub about this part of the question suggests a poor opinion of the intelligence of English newspaper writers or politicians. Is it seriously asked whether the Ministers of a country should have the control of the police of the country? To put the question ought surely to carry its own answer. The Ministers of Ireland will be responsible for the peace and order of Ireland; and Ministers responsible for peace and order, without any force to maintain peace and order, is a more grotesque form of government than, happily for the reputation of humanity, has yet been found to exist in any age or country. If the police were not at the disposal of the Ministers of Ireland, at whose disposal would they be? At the disposal of Downing Street? Then Mr. Parnell, being Prime Minister of Ireland, would be compelled to obtain the consent of the English Ministry before he could order the police to clear a mob who were howling outside College Green; and a riot in Roscommon could not be put down without a Cabinet Council in London, and perhaps a Ministerial crisis at Westminster. Or should the police be at the disposal of some English representative in Ireland? Could there be a more solid guarantee—not for peace and order, but for permanent disturbance and chronic disorder—than a force at the disposal of an alien executive, and with the responsibility for government thus divided between the elected and native rulers and the irresponsible and the foreign representative?

But then it is said the police are fine men, splendidly drilled, well armed—the ideal nucleus of an Irish Army of Independence. If the Irish people would only get as much credit for sanity as for malignity and wickedness, such arguments would scarcely be seriously put forward. It is not alone as an armed garrison that the police are unpopular in Ireland—so far as they are unpopular; it is as men at once highly paid and idle—the well-fed loafers in a land where hideous toil brings bare subsistence; the acceptable suitors for well-dowered beauty; the habitants of well-built and commodious dwellings at the expense of the taxpayers in a land of hovels; the dreamer of pleasant dreams recumbent on trim glass-plots in the long summer days, when the peasant garners scanty crops with perspiring brow. To think that the Irish people would be ready to maintain this vast army of hateful and hated idlers in their poor and penurious land is to show an ignorance of Irish nature that is astounding. As *United Ireland*—not a Whig organ—declared in a recent issue, probably one of the very first acts of an Irish Parliament would be to reduce the constabulary from thirteen thousand to three; to knock the guns out of their hands and replace them with truncheons; and to confine their activity to the discovery of the burglar and the pickpocket, instead of the extinct race of political conspirators.

This fear of separation strikes me as singularly unmanly as well as singularly absurd. One would seriously think that Englishmen had suddenly become convinced that they are a nation of nerveless and backboneless cowards. Will legislative independence widen the Irish Channel or alter the vast disproportion between the populations of England and Ireland? And if the Irish are free to make their own laws; have no irritating interference; if their representatives be safe from the insults and calumnies of dukes and other blackguards; if the Irish nation have the protection of the Empire and few of its burdens; for what, in the name of all that is reasonable, are they to rebel, unless, contrary to experience of the profound Conservatism of the masses of the Irish in America and the Colonies, the Irish are assumed to be a race inevitably and causelessly rebellious?

But the supremacy of an Irish Parliament within the shores of Ireland would imply the robbery of the landlords and the oppression of the so-called Loyal minority. The landlords and the loyal minority are not synonymous and coterminous, as so many English writers seem to think. The two terms mean two very different things. The loyal minority numbers more than a million; the landlords number between five and ten thousand individuals, mostly Protestant, but sometimes Catholic. Now, the protection of the landlords may mean the robbery of the majority of the loyal minority, for the majority of the loyal and Protestant, as well as the so-called seditious and Catholic majority, are tenant-farmers; and measures which would give the landlords more money for their land than it can be made worth to the tenant, would be unjust to the majority of the loyal minority. The Irish Nationalist ought to know no distinction of creed; and it is as much his duty to protect the Orange as it is to protect the Catholic farmer from robbery. And, therefore, the Irish Nationalists would be unfair and dishonest and unjust to the loyal minority as a body by accepting many of the demands put forward by that portion of the loyal minority which consists of the landlords.

The rights of the loyal minority and of the landlords, instead of being identical—so far as property is concerned—are antagonistic. Nor are they entirely identical even as regards religious interests, because, as I have remarked, a large number of the landlords are Catholic. But, still assuming that the landlords, the tenants, and the shopkeepers of the loyal minority are of the same creed, the demand for their protection implies a danger to their religious freedom. The supposition to an Irishman is grotesque. The present leader of the Irish party is a Protestant, and there are four other Protestants in the party: Dr. Tanner, who represents one of the divisions of County Cork, is a Protestant; Mr. Abraham, who represents one of the divisions of Limerick, is a Protestant; Mr. Douglas Pyne, who represents one of the divisions of County Waterford, is a Protestant; and Mr. Jeremiah Jordan, who represents one of the divisions of County Clare, is an Ulster Methodist. Moreover, if this point must really be laboured, the predecessor of Mr. Parnell in the leadership of the Irish party was Mr. Shaw, and he was a Protestant; and his predecessor, again, was Isaac Butt, and he was a Protestant. To speak of any danger to the Protestant's rights of conscience under such circumstances is very absurd. But if the Protestant minority have still any apprehensions, or if their English co-religionists be apprehensive about them, by all means let there be some safeguards for their protection. At the same time two things must be observed: first, that with the exception of the small body of rabid Orangemen who attribute to others the same sanguinary bigotry as they themselves are not ashamed to preach, there is really no section of Irish Protestants who have these unmanly fears, and who do not feel confident that they will be able to maintain the same prominent and important place in the future as they have in the past of Irish life. And secondly, it will be a doubtful boon to the Irish Protestants to put them in any position of isolation from the masses of their countrymen. It will be their interest, as I think it will be generally their desire, to throw in their lot frankly with the rest of their countrymen, with the same rights of exactly equal citizenship.

There remains that which is the real crux of this question—What is to be done with the landlords? Here again an elementary knowledge of the speeches and proposals of the members of the Irish party would do away with some of the bugbears that are frightening English statesmanship. Mr. Parnell has over and over again told the farmers of Ireland that they must fight for the land or pay for the land; and as nobody thinks of fighting for it, of course the farmers were told that they must pay for it. Mr. Parnell was the only politician who ran any serious risk to his popularity or his power in making such a statement, and naturally he made it in good faith. It is pretty clear that the land question must be got out of the way before the national question can be settled. It seems improbable that English opinion will leave the property of the landlords to the disposition of an Irish Parliament, unless, indeed, British Radicalism, in its hatred of the landed aristocracy of this country, might think it desirable to sacrifice the landlords of Ireland, *pour encourager les autres*. This, however, may be dismissed as an unlikely contingency; and the plan which will be probably adopted in the long run will be the purchase out of the landlords by the Irish tenant with the assistance of the English Exchequer. There are many objections to this course, which I cannot go into; but objections must yield to the inevitable, and I believe this solution is inevitable. In the interest alike of the Irish farmer, who has to live off his purchase; in the interest of the British Exchequer, which ought to have ample security for its advance—and the security of the Exchequer will be bad if the bargain of the farmer be foolish—the terms of purchase ought to be arranged on strictly economic and economical principles. It ought to be in the instructions of the Purchase Commissioners that they shall give full credit to the farmer for his improvements, in the spirit of Parliament when it passed the Healy clause; that they will have due regard to the depression of prices, the vicissitudes of British agriculture, the severity of foreign competition; so that the annual payment may not, like the judicial rent, be a fair-weather protection, that breaks down ruinously before the stress of one or two bad seasons.

Finally, there is the guarantee of the Empire from acts directed against its safety and interests. The interference of the Empire ought to have two characteristics: it should be effective, and at the same time it should not be meddlesome or wanton. The way to meet the difficulty which I suggest is a veto by an address of the two Houses of Parliament to the Crown, the address being prefaced by the declaration that the proposed action or legislation of the Irish Parliament is outside the shores of Ireland and the scope of purely Irish affairs; is an interference with the prerogative of the Crown and dangers the safety of the Empire; and should for these reasons be vetoed. The English party system would be a guarantee against wanton or unwise interference. I do not despair of there being men with the Liberal and enlightened spirit of Charles James Fox, in future as in past English Parliaments, to warn against unwise meddling. A settlement on these lines would, I believe, make Ireland prosperous and peaceful and happy, and lead to the strengthening, to the increased dignity and to the better repute of the Empire.

T. P. O'CONNOR.

DR. MATTHEW ROBERTSON.

THE people of Great Britain have a genuine love of freedom, but unfortunately they know but little of the things that have been done and are being done in their name. If the mass of Englishmen and Scotchmen could be accurately informed of the horrible misgovernment which has been carried on in Ireland during the last 700 years, and which in great measure exists even at this moment, they would speedily demand that an end be put to a state of affairs which is disgraceful to England and disastrous to both countries. All the arts of tyranny have been lavishly expended upon "The Sister Isle." Confiscation and robbery in a great variety of forms, massacre, transplanting, bribery, banishment, and starvation, grading up to wholesale extermination, have all been employed with great industry and energy. The cattle trade of Ireland was destroyed to please English landlords, and the Irish colonial trade was crushed to gratify English merchants. Upon the ruins of their cattle trade a people often reproached for lack of energy developed a flourishing woollen industry, and Englishmen blush to read that by an Act of the English Parliament in 1698 this trade was annihilated, and a vast population thrown into utter destitution. Deprived of their industries, and with capital and enterprise banished from the country, the Irish people were flung back on the soil as their only source of livelihood, and from that time to the present hour the favourite form of oppression has been to exact rent for the buildings and improvements which their necessities compelled them to make, and by the aid of legal tricks and quibbles to confiscate their property altogether. Yet after all this there are many people who are surprised that the minds of Irishmen are not overflowing with gratitude for the blessings of English rule. It is true that the darkest days of Ireland are past, but unfortunately the centuries have been bound each to each by consistent bad government. Nations have long memories, and besides, a man has no temptation to forget that his grandfather was hanged for demanding the common rights of citizenship, and that his father was robbed of the proceeds of a long life of toil, when his own back is still sore from the plank bed of coercion, and his footsteps dogged by a Government spy and an armed policeman. The government of Ireland at the present moment is a despotism disguised under parliamentary forms and tempered by obstruction, agitation, and outrages. The mildest and most moderate reforms have again and again been refused by the ignorant prejudices of one House of Parliament and the selfish rapacity of the other. The Land Act of 1881 was a great and just measure, but it could not be passed until evicting and rack-renting landlords went in fear of their lives. Even when it was passed the English House of Lords and the official classes in Ireland have succeeded in depriving it of a great part of its value. Many of the grievances under which Ireland groans, such as the difficulty of forcing local bills at great cost through a lawyer-ridden and lord-ridden Parliament, exist also in England, but in a less aggravated form. But there is a vast field of rank and luxuriant abuses connected with the administration of law which Ireland has all to herself. The Irish executive is composed of the Lord Lieutenant and his chief secretary, who come and go even more swiftly than the party Governments which appoint them. If they are not now taken " wild from Brooks's," as in the days of Lord Northington, they are generally very ignorant of Irish affairs, and fall an easy prey to the permanent officials in Dublin Castle. This reactionary body is maintained in power by some 30,000 soldiers and 12,000 armed police. They treat the people whom they govern with contempt, and are repaid with most intense repugnance. It is by these permanent officials, divided into small committees, that the work of local government, falling under the heads of Local Government Board, Public Works, Prisons Board, Education, &c., is mainly done. The counties are manipulated by means of resident magistrates and the " great unpaid," in neither of whom have the people the smallest confidence.

Perhaps the most important question which statesmen and politicians have to answer at the present moment is whether a good County Government Bill and the abolition of the £10 rating franchise for municipal purposes, together with a complete reform which would put the administration of the law in all its departments in the hands of those who possess the confidence of the Irish people, would be sufficient to effect the pacification of the country and satisfy all reasonable requirements. To that question, after due consideration, the answer must be No, for many reasons, but chiefly the following : The ardent patriotism of the Irish nation has been wounded and lacerated by centuries of oppression, and they will never be satisfied until they have an assembly in Dublin which will fairly embody the idea of self-government in all Irish affairs, and which will provide at once a legitimate object of patriotic sentiment and a worthy arena for Irish genius. Irishmen, moreover, will never be content to administer laws which they regard as unjust, which they did not make, and which they cannot amend. If they attempted to do so, the Irish leaders would discredit themselves with their countrymen, and the people would be more hopelessly discontented than ever. Further, it is only by establishing a national assembly in Dublin that we can get the minority adequately represented, and make the leaders who possess the confidence of some four millions of the Irish people fully responsible for their acts and for the maintenance of law and order. The particular form in which self-government should be given will not only demand but will tax to the utmost all the highest powers of statesmanship. Had our own parliamentary machinery been fairly satisfactory, I should have thought that a scheme of three Grand Committees, one for each of the three countries, composed of all the members for that country, endowed with large and well-defined powers as to local legislation, and sitting for a portion of each year in Dublin, Edinburgh, and London (with perhaps a fourth at Swansea), would have been the most efficient as well as the most palatable scheme. But all plans of this kind break themselves to pieces against that hideous anachronism, a hereditary House of Tory landlords, with an absolute veto on all legislation. The separation of Ireland from England is absolutely out of the question. It was not asked for by Flood, Grattan, or O'Connell, nor is it demanded as yet by the responsible leaders of the Irish people. It would be disastrous to both countries, but chiefly to Ireland. The fiat of Nature has made the union of the two countries as indissoluble and irrevocable as that of Sweden and Norway. This fact is fully recognised by the vast majority of Irishmen, and nothing would prevail to alter that conviction except obstinate and protracted opposition to legitimate demands for Home Rule. We are told that Home Rule would only pave the way to separation, but the danger of separation lies in the hostility and alienation of the Irish people, and these can only be charmed away by granting the fullest measure of local self-government which is consistent with the unity and defence of the Empire. The threats of rebellion made by Orange Tories, who display the quality of their loyalty by threatening to "kick the Queen's crown into the Boyne," are unworthy of serious attention. These fierce individuals have been fed on domination and privilege, and they have secreted spleen and intolerance. But it is probable that, with a cessation of the evil diet, their mental secretions would rapidly improve. The adjustment of the land question is a much more serious difficulty. All honest men on both sides of the Channel would like to see the landlords get a fair, but no more than a fair, compensation. It is admitted that the average reduction of 19 per cent. which has been made on the score of tenants' improvements is totally inadequate in the face of falling prices and failing crops. This fact, together with the tampering with the Healy clause of the Land Act, has made the judicial rents comparatively useless as a basis of valuation. The British taxpayer, who has already paid heavily for the luxury of maintaining a race of rack-renting landlords in Ireland, must not be further taxed for their benefit. The notion that Englishmen should go on denying to a sister nation the primary rights of citizenship, and maintaining at vast expense a huge army to collect rents often cruelly unjust, is a proposal so extravagant that it only needs to be stated to be dismissed.

On the other hand, there are far greater dangers in denying Ireland's claims to self-government than in granting them :

"Hope deferred maketh the heart sick.'

The great body of sensible and moderate men, who would now be amply content with Home Rule, would by refusal be goaded into demanding separation ; there would be renewed disorder and disturbances in Ireland, and the last gleam of confidence in England's justice would disappear. It is very well for a few fire-eaters on the London press to talk lightly of sending over Lord Wolseley to "pacify the country." These inky swashbucklers appear to imagine that Ireland's ills can be promptly cured by Napoleon's "whiff of grapeshot" or another taste of Skeffington's artillery. But Wellington, who was a greater soldier than either Wolseley or Napoleon, knew and confessed that grapeshot and artillery were alike powerless against the passive resistance of a nation determined on obtaining its freedom. Nor do the perils end with disorders in Ireland. In America and in the colonies there are many millions of thriving citizens who are either Irish-born or of Irish parentage. They have carried with them, or have inherited from their parents, bitter memories of cruel and unexpiated wrong. They at least have not forgotten the fact that one million persons perished in Ireland in the famine of 1846, or that of those whom the famine spared nearly a quarter of a million were evicted in the four succeeding years. These men are anxiously watching the attempt to get justice for Ireland by constitutional means, many of them not disguising their hope that it may fail. One of their spokesmen said the other day, amidst the thundering applause of an Irish-American audience, that it was not the question whether Ireland should get her rights, but "whether hell should break out in London," and he left no doubt as to his meaning. "The dynamite," he said, "which England has used to crush weak nations and struggling patriots in various parts of the world, we will use against her, if she refuses to our country the freedom which is her right." At this crisis in our history the eyes of the whole nation, and indeed of the whole world, are turned to one man. Mr. Gladstone saved Ireland to the

Empire once before by the Alabama arbitration. Let him save it once again by a bold and just measure of Home Rule. He will hear much of what is feasible and what is popular; but every enlightened lover of his country would wish him to turn a deaf ear to empty and ignorant clamour, and ask him to put before the country, not the scheme which may be most popular for the moment, but the scheme which is absolutely the best of which the nature of the case admits. Let him expound the bearings of the question as only he can expound them; let him make his appeal to that higher and better nature of the British people to which he has never appealed in vain; and it will come to pass that to such a scheme, founded alike on nature and on justice, the best men both in Ireland and Great Britain will steadily rally. He will show that trust in the people is a Liberal principle, which applies to Ireland as well as to England, and he will crown a career rendered illustrious by great achievements by the greatest and most beneficent of them all, by a measure which shall restore peace and prosperity to Ireland, and give stability and safety to the Empire.

MATTHEW ROBERTSON.

THE LORD MAYOR OF DUBLIN.

(RIGHT HON. T. D. SULLIVAN, M.P.)

I THINK the wise thing and the first thing for England to do is to allow the Irish people to manage their own local affairs. England has had the management of them for centuries, and the results are—poverty, discontent, disaffection, Coercion Acts, attempted rebellions, and all sorts of trouble in Ireland.

These are just the things that a similar system of government would produce among any other people in the world.

The irritation against England, the so-called "disloyalty," the desire of revenge upon her felt by masses of the Irish people, would assuredly abate if the conditions of life for them in their own country were made more tolerable and more honourable.

Never will they willingly submit to such domination over their affairs as England has been exercising hitherto. If many of them desire separation, what wonder, when the connection is humiliating, injurious, and consequently hateful to them?

Make it pleasant, or at all events harmless, to them; allow them the fair and reasonable right of control over the internal affairs of their own country; and by a law of Nature the strain between the two countries would cease. The ill-feeling would decline, and the interests which they have in common would operate to make them good neighbours and friends.

I hope we are near a settlement of the trouble. If not, all I can say is, that I believe the longer it is delayed the worse it will be for England—perhaps for both countries.

T. D. SULLIVAN.

MICHAEL DAVITT.

THE question is frequently asked, "What will satisfy the Irish people?" And the answer is as frequently volunteered, "Nothing. Nothing will satisfy them but total separation—and that they won't get." It is an illogical way of answering a question, but pardonable in an Englishman; and the impatience which it manifests is also strikingly characteristic. Your ordinary Englishman entertains the pretty conceit that English rule is of such a beneficent character that any people who do not tamely submit to it are to be pitied and—dragooned. While in particular, the Irish people, for their obstinacy in refusing to see any virtue in English rule in Ireland, "must be clearly made to understand," and "must be told once for all," that England will maintain her hold upon Ireland at all costs. All this talk is indulged in really for the sake of concealing the chagrin which England experiences in consequence of the fact, revealed in recent years, that the people of Ireland have discovered how to make it more difficult for England to rule Ireland, than to govern all the rest of her vast empire put together. English statesmen, even now, are devising a middle course between things as they are, and total separation. They are casting about for a scheme which will combine the characteristics of modern statesmanship—a scheme, for example, which will involve as small a concession as possible to the demand of the people concerned, and have a fair chance of passing the House of Lords. Eminent statesmen have more than once challenged Irish public men to say what they want, but the required answer has not been forthcoming. There have been answers, but they have been too reasonable. English statesmen have not been able to offer upon them the comment, "We told you so, the thing demanded is utterly out of the range of practical politics, and, in point of fact, is absolutely out of the question." The answer really required is such a one as English statesmen can meet with a *non possumus*. And for this reason, English statesmen, I repeat, know that a substantial concession will have to be made to the genius of Irish nationality within the next few years. The demand for it is too strong to be resisted; for the Irish race have to be dealt with now. If at home on Irish soil the people can "make the ruling powers uneasy" to such an extent as I have indicated, in Westminster their representatives can clog the wheels of legislation and endanger the very existence of Government by parliamentary methods; while abroad, in Great Britain, America, Australia, Canada, the exiled Irish have discovered how to operate on the flank, so to speak, by elevating the Irish question into the position of a national or colonial issue. Further, England's guilt towards Ireland is known and commented on all over the world. Further still, the real people of England—the working men of England— have of late been asking for the reasons why Ireland should be perpetually discontented, and the answers they have received, to the credit of their common sense, be it said, do not appear to have satisfied them. Respectable England is very angry; and, to conceal their annoyance at the inevitable, and to pave the way for a concession, English statesmen ask the question of Irish public men—" What do you want?" and require an answer to which they may return an emphatic "impossible." But this is only diplomacy. They only desire us to say how much we want, in order to say in reply how little they will give. They ask us to "formulate our demand," that they, in formulating their concession, may assure their opponents of its comparative innocence. Responsible Irish public men have declined to fall into the trap. And they have acted very wisely. For why should Irish public men show their hand rather than English Prime Ministers?

Apart altogether from considerations of this character, however, there are others of a distinctly Irish nature which the leaders of the National movement in Ireland have to take into account. The varying shades of National sentiment may not be ignored. Let us therefore analyse the degrees of intensity of Irish Nationalist aspirations.

We have first, the Extremists, those who believe that total separation from England is the only thing that would satisfy Irish genius or develop it properly. These include the most self-sacrificing Irishmen. They represent, in their aspirations for Irish liberty, those who have made the most illustrious names in Ireland's history. They include many cultured men, especially among the expatriated portion of the race, but their main strength is in the working classes. Patriotism is purer among the industrial order because less modified by mercenary motives and less liable to corrupting influences. But the Extremists or Separatists are divided among themselves upon the question of method. There are Separatists who advocate physical force, believing moral force—that is, constitutional means, ineffectual and demoralizing. This section includes men who have never tried moral force, and who believe solely either in "honourable warfare" or "dynamite." It also includes those who have tried moral force, and given it up in despair. Then there are the Separatists, who, with the experiences of '48 and '67 before their minds, rely upon constitutional action alone.

Next in importance to the Extremists come the Home Rulers, or Federalists, who may be divided into those who disbelieve in the possibility of Separation and those who do not see its necessity. This section of the National party includes some of the ablest and most earnest men in Ireland. Their methods, I need hardly say, are strictly constitutional.

No Irish leader can afford to ignore either of these two principal phases of Irish National sentiment. Were such a man to commit himself to a definite scheme, at the mere invitation of an English Minister, he would run the risk of alienating that section of his supporters whose views were not represented in his proposals. It is an obvious remark that such a contingency would not be unwelcome to English statesmen. From what I have just said, it will be readily perceived how difficult is the task to which Irish popular leaders are asked to address themselves.

Nevertheless, I shall venture to outline a scheme of local and National self-government which, I believe, would command the support of the majority of the Irish people at home and abroad, and which would probably receive a fair trial at the hands of the Extremists; though its operation would undoubtedly be watched with a jealous eye.

In the first place, there should be established in Ireland a system of county government, by means of Elective Boards, to take the place of the existing unrepresentative and practically irresponsible Grand Jury system. The functions of such Boards should be more comprehensive than those exercised by the Grand Juries. For example, in addition to the duty of administering purely county business these Boards should be permitted to initiate measures of general application; such as schemes of arterial drainage, tramways, railways, canals, docks, harbours, and similar enterprises, which would be of more than local importance and character. Such schemes, after being fully discussed by these elective bodies, would be submitted to the National Assembly to be subsequently described. Then the County Boards should control the police within the county, and appoint the magistrates, and be entirely responsible for the preservation of law and order.

Further, should the land problem be justly and satisfactorily solved on the lines of national proprietary, the duty of assessing and collecting the land-tax would naturally devolve upon the County Boards, which, deducting what was necessary for the expenses of county government, would remit the balance to the National Exchequer. In fact, the object of such a system should be to constitute each county, as far as practicable, a self-governing community.

Manifestly any system of local self-government for Ireland involves a corresponding one of National self-government as its natural and inevitable complement. To extend the principle of local self-government at all in Ireland, without radically changing the system of Castle rule, would only have the effect of increasing the friction already existing between the people and their rulers. Hence, it is absolutely necessary that legislation for National self-government should go hand in hand with any scheme for the creation of Elective County Boards. I am well aware that the hope is indulged, in some quarters, that the inclusion of Ireland in a general measure of county government, with the sop of an Irish Parliamentary Grand Committee thrown in, will suffice to choke off the demand for Irish legislative independence; but English statesmen need not delude themselves with the idea that any such Westminster expedient will satisfy the genius of Irish Nationality.

There could be established in Dublin a National

Assembly composed of elected members from the constituencies of Ireland, who should proceed to the administration of all Irish affairs in the manner which obtains in colonial parliaments, excepting the substitution of one for two Chambers, here proposed. That is to say, the Representative of the Crown in Ireland would call upon some member of the National Assembly to form a government, the different members of which should be constituted the heads of the various Boards, which at present are practically irresponsible bureaucracies; but which, under the system here proposed, would become departments of a popular government, and open to the supervision of the people through the National Assembly. Such a government, subject to the control of the governed through their elected representatives, would be the practical solution of the Anglo-Irish difficulty. It would be but the common definition of constitutional rule carried into practice. It would, as already remarked, be the application to misgoverned and unfortunate Ireland of a constitution kindred to that which British statesmanship has long since granted, wisely and well, to a consequently peaceful and contented Canada.

Certainly if a similar act of political justice and sound policy does not solve the Irish difficulty, nothing less will. What possible danger could England run from such an application of constitutional rule to a country much nearer to the centre of Imperial power than Canada? But what a beneficent change for Ireland—nay, what a relief to England herself—would be involved in such an act of simple political justice!

MICHAEL DAVITT.

A SKETCH OF IRISH HISTORY.

By JUSTIN HUNTLY McCARTHY, M.P.

IRELAND can boast of ancient legends rivalling in beauty and in dignity the tales of Attica and Argolis ; she has an early history whose web of blended myth and reality is as richly coloured as the record of the rulers of Alba Longa and the story of the Seven Kings. She may be proud of the grandeur of her ecclesiastical chronicle ; she may rejoice in her illustrious roll of saints, and dwell fondly upon the memory of days when her island was the centre of Western scholarship, the head water from which the missionary streams of Christian civilization flowed over Europe. For the moment, however, and for my present purpose, the history of Ireland begins with the twelfth century and the arrival of the Norman knights. Important though that history is, it has too often been curiously neglected by many who speak lightly upon the great question which has sprung from it. I propose therefore to give here the briefest outline of the history of Ireland, so that the reader may at least know something of the succession of events, and have before him a scheme into which he can fit such further knowledge as he may care to acquire.

In the twelfth century, all Ireland, with the exception of certain Danish seaport settlements, was divided amongst Irish chiefs of ancient lineage, who quarrelled and fought and made peace with each other like the heads of the petty

Grecian States. More than one English monarch had dreamt of adding the neighbour island to the appanages of the Norman Crown; an English pontiff gave the excuse for making the dream reality. Nicholas Breakspere, the only Englishman who ever sat in the seat of St. Peter, known among the popes as Adrian IV., gave Henry II. a Bull of authority over Ireland. For some years the English king made no use of the English pope's permission.

The whole story of the seven centuries of struggle between Ireland and England begins with the carrying off of Devorgilla, wife of Tiernan O'Rourke of Brefny, by a sexagenarian ruffian, Dermot Macmurrough, King of Leinster. The lord of Brefny raised a league of princes against his wronger; Dermot fled from Ireland to Aquitaine, laid his allegiance at Henry's feet and implored his aid. Henry permitted Dermot to shark up a list of landless resolutes, who, headed by Richard de Clare, Earl of Pembroke, called Strongbow, invaded Ireland.

At first the Normans carried all before them. Suddenly Dermot died; the Irish plucked up heart, and began to harass their enemies seriously. Henry, jealous of the triumphs of his subordinates, seemed little inclined to lend them help. Strongbow, however, succeeded in soothing his king, who led over a large army to Ireland, on what Sir John Davies afterwards called a *Veni, Vidi, Vici*, visit.

Overawed by this armament, many of the Irish chiefs "came in" and submitted. Henry, without interfering with those that still held out, set to work to organize his new territory. He divided it into counties, and set up Courts of Bench, Pleas, and Exchequer in Dublin, to give his Normans the privilege of English law, while the Irish were still permitted to adhere to their antique Brehon laws.

The history of Ireland from the first to the second

Richard is one monotonous record of battle between the Normans and the Irish, and of strife between the rival Irish houses. The Norman barons lived like little kings in their own domains, lords of life and death, ruling their subjects with a queer mixture of Brehon and Norman law, after their own fashion, eternally assailing and assailed by the Irish. Only the members of five specified Irish houses could have audience in the English courts of justice. The killing of an Irishman or the violation of an Irishwoman by a Norman colonist was no crime.

Gradually, however, Irish influences began to act upon the foreigners. The Normans began to seek to be at peace with their Irish neighbours, to marry Irish wives, even to adopt Irish names, dress, languages, and law. The English Government at home dreaded this process of assimilation, and strove to check it. A law of 1295 forbade the adoption of the Irish garb by Norman settlers. A law of 1356 declared that no one born in Ireland should hold any of the king's towns or castles. In 1367 a Parliament at Kilkenny prescribed heavy penalties for all Normans adopting Irish names, speech, or customs, maintaining Irish bards, or fostering Norman with Irish children. The Norman who married an Irish wife was to forfeit his estate, to be half hanged, shamefully mutilated, and disembowelled alive.

But these fierce laws were for the time impotent. The Anglo-Irish barons still intermarried, still blended with the Irish houses. Of all the Anglo-Irish families the most powerful were the Geraldines, descendants of a companion of Strongbow, who had come to be spoken of as more Irish than the Irish themselves. In the time of Henry VII. the actual English colony, the Pale, was reduced within very narrow limits, and the greater part of the island was in the hands of Irish or Anglo-Irish chieftains, who defied the repeated and powerless renewals of the statutes of Kilkenny.

Henry VII. was at first content to let Ireland alone, and to tacitly recognize the authority of the Geraldines ; but when the Geraldines, who were staunch Yorkists, fostered the causes of Warbeck and Simnel, he retaliated with "curious cruelty" by striking at the legislative freedom of Ireland.

Up to 1494 no attempt had been made to force English law upon the Irish septs, or to interfere with the self-government of the Norman settlers. The Norman Parliament in Ireland, though a poor thing enough, did contain the principles of a representative system. Originally a kind of council of barons and prelates, it had grown into greater importance, had its Upper and Lower House, and passed its own laws. In 1494, Sir Edward Poyning, backed by a great army, changed the relationship between the two islands. In a Parliament at Drogheda, Poyning's Act was passed. This Act declared that all English laws should operate in Ireland, and that the consent of the English Privy Council was necessary to all Acts of the Irish Parliament. This deprivation of Ireland's right to independent government has been the chief source of the trouble and disaffection of four centuries.

Under Henry VIII. the power of the Geraldines was shattered, and their noblest lords perished at Tyburn. Henry's reforming zeal confiscated the Church lands in Ireland, as they had been confiscated in England. He further strengthened the hold of the English Crown on Ireland by summoning a Parliament in Dublin, at which submissive Irish chiefs sat for the first time side by side with English barons, which conferred on Henry and his successors the title of King, instead of Lord Paramount of Ireland.

The process of reformation and of aggression, begun by Henry VIII. and carried on with pitiless determination against unfaltering opposition by Edward VI., was renewed, after a brief period of respite under Mary, by Queen Elizabeth. Shane O'Neil, head of the House of Tyrone, stood out against her successfully for a time, but at last he was killed by treachery, and hordes of English immigrants poured on to his escheated lands. Against these inroads the great Geraldine League was formed. One child of the ancient house had escaped from the wholesale massacre of his race, and had been allowed by Mary to resume his ancestral honours. The Geraldines were once more a powerful family in Ireland; they got encouragement in Rome and pledges from Spain, and they rose against the English rule. They had many wrongs to avenge. Elizabeth's officers had been slaughtering mercilessly, and, as in the case of Cosby of Mullaghmast, often treacherously, the heads and the followings of the great Irish houses. The rebellious Geraldines had a temporary success; then their fortunes faded again, and the rebellion was put down with the strong hand. Its leaders died on the field or rotted in the Tower. Munster was so desolated by fire and sword that, in the words of Mr. Froude, "the lowing of a cow or the sound of a ploughboy's whistle was not to be heard from Valentia to the Rock of Cashel. Pacified Munster was divided into Crown lands, held in fee by such adventurers as cared to struggle with the outlawed Irish.

A steady succession of dragoonings and confiscations raised up a new enemy to Elizabeth in Hugh O'Neil, a young chief of Tyrone who had been brought up at the English Court, but who was finally forced into rebellion by the harsh treatment inflicted upon his kinsmen. For a time Tyrone was successful; in the end he was defeated and forced to come to terms, by which he completely submitted to the English Crown and promised to introduce English laws and customs into Tyrone. Elizabeth was dead and

James I. king when these terms were concluded. But Tyrone and his kinsman of Tyrconnell, even when defeated and submissive, still were obstacles in the way of James's policy of reform in Ireland. In King James's mind reform meant the fierce enforcement of the Protestant faith, the relentless proscription of the Catholic creed, the destruction of all Irish law and custom, and the comprehensive annexation of the estates of Irish chiefs. Tyrone and Tyrconnell were in his way; they were conveniently accused of treason; they had no means of resistance; they fled across the seas to France first, and afterwards to Rome, where they died; and travellers to-day may stand by their worn graves in St. Pietro of Montorio, on the Janiculum.

The Flight of the Earls left Ireland entirely in James's hands. There were strong English settlements in Leinster, Connaught, and Munster; similar settlements were made in Ulster. The Limavaddy Commission dealt out the confiscated lands of the followers of Tyrone and Tyrconnell to City of London companies. Fraud as well as force was called in to aid in disinheriting Irish landowners. Men called "Discoverers" found a profitable occupation in hunting out flaws in titles of land, that they might be confiscated to the Crown. Infamous adventurers like Richard Boyle, who was afterwards the first Earl of Cork, swarmed over the country, patronized by their king and hated by the Irish, over whom they were set up as masters. Charles I. carried on his parent's processes of plantation as systematically as his father. With the fall of Charles many of the Irish thought their time had come. In 1641 the remnant of native Irish in Ulster rose, under Sir Phelim O'Neil, against the oppression of the Scotch settlers. This rising of 1641 has been made the most of by English historians of the school of Mr. Froude. The average English writer on Irish history apparently loses his head in sheer amazement at the discovery that the Irish broke the monotony of the wrongs of half a dozen reigns and the oppression of many generations by a rising, in which the rebels killed some of their oppressors, as their oppressors had always killed them and theirs whenever they could get at them. The Irish had been robbed, cheated, outlawed, murdered, exiled, sold into foreign service, treated as slaves and worse than beasts; and yet when they turned upon their torturers, the indignation of English historians is only one degree greater than their surprise. I have no wish—no one can wish—to excuse any crimes that accompanied the rising of 1641, but it must be remembered that most nations, like most human beings, who have been treated cruelly, are cruel in their revenge when they get it, and the followers of Sir Phelim O'Neil had the cruellest wrongs to avenge. If they did slay, they had learned hideous lessons of slaughter from their masters. The massacre of Mullaghmast, the massacre of the clan O'Neil by Essex, the dragooning of Connaught, the desolation of Munster, the shameful slaughter at Smerwick, are lightly ignored by English historians, in order to lend an uncontrasted horror to the violences of 1641.

Sir Phelim O'Neil's rising soon flamed into general rebellion. Owen Roe O'Neil came over from Spain to lead the insurgent forces. Smooth success at first was strewn before his feet. A national convention met at Kilkenny in October 1642 to establish the independence of Ireland. Then Cromwell entered Ireland, and carried all before him. Were what has been said of the massacre of 1641 true, it pales into pitiful insignificance by the side of the wholesale slaughter done in Cromwell's name and by Cromwell's orders. Drogheda and Wexford put the fables about Portadown wholly into the shade. Owen Roe died, poisoned it was said; Sir Phelim O'Neil was captured and executed; the rebellion was over, and Cromwell proceeded with a free hand to parcel Ireland out once more among aliens by race and aliens by religion.

While the struggle was going on the English Parliament had stimulated the zeal of its officers and soldiers, and acquired the monetary support of speculating adventurers with liberal debentures on the as yet unconquered Irish land. The majority of the happy holders of these bonds, however, objected to settling in their promised land till all danger of aggression from the turbulent dispossessed was over. Accordingly more than forty thousand of the disbanded Irish soldiery were forced into foreign service. Irish women and girls were shipped off by thousands into shameful slavery, for the consolation of West Indian planters weary of maroon or negro women and of the soldiery in the newly acquired colony of Jamaica.

Even after these wholesale deportations the adventurers were so fearful for their own safety, and the Government so careful of them, that each of the planted counties was divided in half, and settlements of civilian adventurers alternated with soldier settlements, to keep them free of all Irish influences. Connaught was set apart for the Irish, and into Connaught the Irish were driven and cooped. The Irish in Connaught were treated like prisoners in Siberia: they might not come within two miles of the river or four of the sea; a passport system was established, any evasion of which meant death without form of trial. Irish noblemen were compelled to wear a distinctive mark upon their dress under pain of death. Men of lower rank bore a black spot on the right cheek, under pain of branding and even hanging. Slaughter, starvation, and transportation thinned still further the reduced numbers of the transplanted Irish. The Irish merchants were ruthlessly ejected from the great towns, almost without compensation, to make room for English merchants from Liverpool or Gloucester. The Irish merchants carried their skill and thrift across the seas, and the cuckoo-cloud of foreign settlers were unable to keep up the prosperity of the violated cities. Such of the contumacious and ungrateful Irish as would neither hang, transplant, nor fly into exile, took to the mountains, and lived a life of guerilla warfare, like the Klephts of Greece. The English Government put a price alike upon the heads of these fugitives, of Catholic priests and of wolves. Yet all these " precautions " failed to preserve the settlers intact from Irish influences, and less than half a century later many of the children of Cromwell's Ironsides could not speak a word of English.

The Restoration brought little advantage with it, even to those dispossessed Irish who owed their ruin to their adhesion to the House of Stuart. It was more advantageous to Charles to confirm the Cromwellian settlements than to reinstate the Irish lords, and accordingly, except in the rarest cases, the plundered Irish were unable to win back a rood of land from the new men. Even the persecution of the Catholics did not cease, for Charles's tendency towards toleration was checked by the fury of the Titus Oates' plot. Under James, indeed, the treatment of the Catholics changed for the better, and in consequence the war between James and William of Orange found the Irish Catholics, under Talbot of Tyrconnell, fighting on the Stuart side.

James met this allegiance with many concessions. Poyning's Act was formally repealed. A measure was passed restoring the dispossessed Irish to their lands. But at Limerick the hopes of the Stuarts and of the Irish Catholics were alike extinguished. The city was so well defended by Patrick Sarsfield against fearful odds, that he forced from his enemies a treaty providing that the Catholics of Ireland should enjoy religious freedom, and giving King James's followers the right to their estates. The treaty was signed, the city was surrendered, Sarsfield and his soldiers marched out with all the honours of war and went into foreign service, and then the treaty was broken. The ink was scarcely dried upon the parchment before the King and his Ministers violated all its pledges. The forfeited lands were reconfiscated, and sold by auction, as before, to English corporations and adventurers. Even more shamelessly was faith broken with the Irish as Catholics. William was determined to make Ireland Protestant by penal laws.

Up to this time Catholics had sat among the Lords and Commons of the Irish Parliament. When the first Irish Parliament after the surrender of Limerick met in 1692, an oath was framed by the Protestant majority and presented to all members of the House alike. A special oath to be administered to Roman Catholics had been duly provided for in the treaty. The new parliamentary oath was fashioned with horrible ingenuity to insult and outrage every Catholic. The Catholic Peers and Commons quitted the two Houses in indignation. From that hour, for more than a century, until the Parliament itself ceased to exist, no Catholic Irishman sat in his country's senate.

All obstacles being thus removed, the penalizing process went on briskly. But the work of William's reign, with all its hatred of the Catholics and its malign ingenuity in injuring them, was not comprehensive enough to satisfy the statesmen of the reign of Anne. What was begun under William received additions under the first and even under the third George. But it is to the ten years which embrace the last lustre of the seventeenth and the first lustre of the eighteenth century that the penal laws particularly belong. It is not necessary now—it is terrible to think that it ever could have been necessary—to waste any words in condemnation of these measures. The eloquence of Burke, the genius of Fox, cannot add one stain to the shame, or one sting to the horror of the bare recital of what these laws sought to do.

It was laid down from the bench, by Lord Chancellor Bowes and Chief Justice Robinson, that the law did not suppose any such person to exist as an Irish Roman Catholic. Dopping, Bishop of Meath, declared from the pulpit that Protestants were not bound to keep faith with Papists. The penal laws did their best to justify Bowes and Robinson by insuring that no such person as an Irish Catholic should exist. In their own country Catholics were excluded from every civil or military profession, from every Government office, from the highest to the lowest, and from almost every duty and privilege of a citizen. They could not sit in the Irish Parliament, or vote members to it. They were excluded from the army and navy, the corporations, the magistracy, the bar, the bench, the grand juries, and the vestries. They could not be sheriffs or soldiers, gamekeepers or constables. They were forbidden to own arms, and any two justices or sheriffs might at any time issue a search warrant for arms. The discovery of any kind of weapon rendered its Catholic owner liable to fines, imprisonment, whipping, or the pillory. They could not own a horse worth more than five pounds, and any Protestant tendering that sum could compel his Catholic neighbour to sell his animal. They were allowed no education whatever. A Catholic could not go to the university; he might not be the guardian of a child; he might not keep a school, or send his children to be educated abroad, or teach them himself. Every Catholic priest pursued his sacred calling under a penalty of death. Every Catholic refusing to attend Protestant worship could be heavily fined, dispossesed of his land, and even banished for life. No Catholic might buy land, or inherit or receive it as a gift from Protestants, or hold life annuities or leases for more than thirty-one years, or any lease on such terms as that the profits of the land exceeded one-third the value of the land. If a Catholic purchased an estate, the first Protestant who informed against him became its proprietor. The eldest son of a Catholic, upon apostatising, became heir-at-law to the whole estate of his father, and reduced his father to the position of a mere life tenant. A wife who apostatised was immediately freed from her husband's control, and assigned a certain proportion of her husband's property. Any child, however young, who professed to be a Protestant, was at once taken from his father's care, and a certain proportion of his father's property assigned to him. Any marriage between a Catholic and a Protestant was, by the fact of the husband and wife being of opposite faiths, null and void, without any process of law whatever. A man might leave his wife, or a woman her husband, after twenty years of marriage, in such a case, and bring a legal bastardy on all their offspring.

The statutory destruction of Irish trade supplemented the crimes of the penal code. Under Charles I. Stafford had done his best to ruin the Irish woollen manufacturers in order to benefit the English clothiers. Under Charles II. the importation of Irish cattle, or sheep, or swine was prohibited. In 1663 Ireland was left out of the Act for the encouragement of trade, so that all the carrying trade in Irish-built ships within any part of his Majesty's dominions was prevented. But it was reserved for William to do the worst. In 1696 all direct trade from Ireland with the English colonies was forbidden, and a revival of the woollen trade was crushed by an Act which prohibited the export of Irish wool or woollen goods from any Irish port except Cork, Drogheda, Dublin, Kinsale, Waterford, and Youghal, to any port in the world except Milford, Chester, Liverpool, and certain ports in the Bristol Channel, under a penalty of £500 and the forfeiture of both ship and cargo.

It has been truly said that during the greater part of the eighteenth century Ireland has no history. Ferocity and famine allied to crush the country into quiescent misery. Neither in 1715 nor in 1745 had the Irish Catholics the strength to raise a hand for the Pretenders. The secret societies which came into existence among the peasantry are the only evidence of anything like active opposition to the reign of terror. But bad as the condition of Ireland was, the English Government aimed at making it worse by depriving it of its last remains of legislative independence. The abolition of the Irish Parliament was dreamt of in the early years of Anne. Its independence was enfeebled in the sixth year of George the First by an Act which not only deprived the Irish House of Lords of any appellate jurisdiction, but declared that the English Parliament had the right to make laws to bind the people of the kingdom of Ireland. The "heads of a Bill" might indeed be brought in in either Irish House. If agreed to, they were carried to the Viceroy, who gave them to his Privy Council, to alter if they chose, and send to England. They were subject to alteration by the English Attorney-General, and when approved by the English Privy Council, sent back to Ireland, where the Irish Houses could either accept or reject them *in toto*, but had no power to change them.

The Irish Parliament in the eighteenth century was a mere caricature of a legislative body. In its Upper House many of the temporal Peers were Englishmen or Scotchmen, some of whom had never even set foot in Ireland. The actual Irishmen on its roll were mostly the corrupt purchasers of degraded titles. Its spiritual Peers, foreign to the country by religion and by race, were so obnoxious, even to men of that religion and that race, as to wring from Swift the satirical declaration, that all the Irish bishops appointed in England must have been murdered on their way by highwaymen, who stole their garments and filled their offices in Dublin.

The Lower House was little better. It was in no sense a representative chamber. " Of three hundred members," said Grattan, " above two hundred are returned by individuals ; from forty to fifty are returned by ten persons ; several of your boroughs have no resident elector at all ; some of them have but one ; and on the whole, two-thirds of the representatives in the House of Commons are returned by less than one hundred persons." Seats were bought and sold like peerages and other articles of contemporary merchandise. It was crowded with supple placemen of the Government, in a proportion of more than a third of the whole body, who were well rewarded for their obedient votes ; it was torn by factions, which the Government ingeniously played off against each other ; its majority, as Grattan showed, was made up of nominees of the Protestant landlords. The Opposition could never turn out the Administration, for the Administration was composed of the irremovable and irreponsible Lords Justices of the Privy Council and certain officers of State. The Opposition, such as it was, was composed of Jacobites, who dreamed of a Stuart restoration, and of a few men animated by a patriotic belief in their country's rights.

The patriot party in and out of Parliament contains some of the most illustrious names in Ireland's history. Swift, Molyneux, Lucas (the founder of the *Freeman's Journal*), Flood, Grattan, Charlemont, Hussey Burgh, Daly, each in his turn and time sustained the enfeebled and fainting cause of Irish nationality.

The war with the American colonies gave Grattan, then leader of the Patriot party in the Parliament, the opportunity of realizing his ambition of securing the legislative independence of his country. A large force of volunteers had been organized in Ireland to guard the country against American attack, and the volunteers were entirely in sympathy with the Patriots. The volunteers formed a convention to express the national grievances; England, occupied by Mr. Washington and his rebels, gave way; the hated Act of George the First was repealed, and Grattan was able to wish a free people and a disenthralled Parliament a perpetual existence.

The free Irish Parliament promised to show itself worthy of its creator. It gave the Irish Catholics the right to vote which had been so long denied them; there is no doubt that it would in time have allowed Catholics to enter Parliament. But Grattan's effort after Catholic Emancipation failed; the volunteers had been disbanded, and were no longer at his back; and a new and more ambitious organization had come into existence.

The name "United Irishmen" designated a number of men all over the country who had formed themselves into clubs for the purpose of promoting a union of friendship between Irishmen of every religious persuasion, and of forwarding a full, fair, and adequate representation of all the people in Parliament. It was in the beginning a perfectly loyal body, with a Protestant gentleman, Mr. Hamilton Rowan, for its president, and James Napper Tandy, a Protestant Dublin trader, for its secretary. The men who created it were well pleased with the success of Grattan's efforts at the independence of the Irish Parliament, but they were deeply discontented at the subsequent disbandment of the volunteers and Grattan's comparative inaction. The simple repeal of the sixth George did not answer their aspirations for liberty, which were encouraged and excited by the outbreak of the French Revolution. Their chief leaders were Theobald Wolfe Tone, a young barrister—brave, adventurous, and eloquent; Lord Edward Fitzgerald; and Arthur O'Connor, Lord Longueville's nephew, and member for Phillipstown. They were all young; they were all Protestants; they were all dazzled by the successes of the French Revolution, and believed that the House of Hanover might be as easily overturned in Ireland as the House of Capet had been in France.

Wolfe Tone went over to Paris, and won the sympathy of the French Directory. A French fleet under Hoche was sent to Ireland, only to be dispersed by storm without effecting a landing. The Government, familiar through spies with the plans of the United Irishmen, struck at its leaders. Arthur O'Connor was arrested and banished; Edward Fitzgerald was captured after a fierce struggle, and died of his wounds in prison; Wolfe Tone was seized later, and died mysteriously in prison, murdered according to some, a suicide according to others. The great insurrection which was to have shattered the power of England was converted into a series of untimely abortive local risings, of which the most successful took place in Wexford. It was crushed out with pitiless severity, until the deeds of the English soldiers and yeomanry became hateful in the eyes of the Viceroy himself, Lord Cornwallis.

It should be borne in mind, in considering the rebellion of 1798, that the struggle is not to be considered as a struggle of creed against creed. Protestants began and organized the movement. Among the leaders of the United Irishmen, Catholics were only in the proportion of one to four throughout the rebellion. On the other hand, a large number of Catholics were strongly opposed to the rebellion, and in many cases took active measures against it. In Wexford, unhappily, the efforts of the Orangemen succeeded in giving the struggle there much of the character of a religious war, but this the revolution as a whole never was. It was a national movement, an uprising against intolerable grievances, and it was sympathized with and supported by Irishmen of all religious denominations, bound together by common injuries and a common desire to redress them.

Having destroyed the revolution, the Government promptly resolved to destroy the Parliament. The ruin of the Irish Parliament is one of the most shameful stories of corruption and treachery of which history holds witness. It was necessary to obtain a Government majority in the Irish Parliament, and the majority was manufactured by the most unblushing bribery. Place and office were lavishly distributed. Peerages won the highest and secret service money the lowest of those who were to be bought. The Bill of Union was introduced and passed by a well-paid majority of sixty in 1800. Grattan pleaded to the last against the unholy pact; but the speech of angels would have been addressed in vain to the base and venal majority. It is something to remember that a hundred men could be found even in that degraded assembly whom the Ministry could not corrupt, and who were faithful to the end to the constitutional liberties of their country.

The history of Ireland since 1800 is one succession of protests, either by arms or by constitutional agitation, against the Union, and of incessant attempts on the part of the Government to keep the Irish in the semblance of content by coercive legislation. The rising of Robert Emmet in 1803; the great Repeal agitation of Daniel O'Connell; the wild, poetic, hopeless insurrection of Young Ireland in 1848; the Phœnix Conspiracy; the Fenian Brotherhood and the rising of 1867; the Home Rule agitation of 1870, which has grown into the present great national and constitutional demand, expressed in the persons of eighty-six represen-

L

tatives at Westminster—these are all links in the historic chain of hatred of the Union—are all but different expressions of the nation's desire for that self-government of which it was so unjustly deprived. Those eighty-six years record also the partial settlement of certain Irish grievances, concessions grudgingly and tardily granted in the unsuccessful hope of making the Irish people indifferent to their stolen constitutional liberties. The horrible story of the Tithe war, over which so much blood was spilt and so much money squandered, is in a measure compensated for by the final Disestablishment of the so-called Irish Church. The Emancipation of the Catholics was conceded at last when the choice lay between concession and civil war. The fearful famine years from 1845 to 1847, which killed their thousands and sent thousands more into exile across the Atlantic, and the incessant evictions which drove the people into never-ceasing emigration, and enabled the *Times* to boast that in a few years a Celtic Irishman would be as rare in Connemara as a Red Indian on the shores of Manhattan, had at least the effect of building up a new Irish nation in the States of the American Union. The rack-rent, the eviction, and the Ribbon lodge were the bitter seed which blossomed in the Land Acts of 1860, of 1870, and of 1881.

But while the expressed discontent of Ireland with the Union has waxed and waned, while the ceaseless misery of the Irish people has varied in intensity, while the satisfaction of her crying needs has been fitfully conceded, one thing has remained incessant, unvaried, uninterupted : this was coercive legislation. Roughly speaking, the country from 1800 to 1885 has never been governed by the ordinary law. From 1796 to 1802 an Insurrection Act was in force, and from 1797 to 1802 the Habeas Corpus Act was suspended. From 1803 to 1805 the country was under martial law; and from the same year to 1806 Habeas Corpus was suspended. Insurrection Acts were in force from 1807 to 1810, from 1814 to 1818, from 1822 to 1825. Habeas Corpus was again suspended in 1822 to 1823. In 1829, in the debate on Catholic Emancipation, Sir Robert Peel was able to say that "for scarcely a year during the period that has elapsed since the Union has Ireland been governed by the ordinary course of law." From the date of that utterance to the present day the country has scarcely been governed by the ordinary law for a single year. Arms Acts, suspensions of Habeas Corpus, changes of venue, Peace Preservation Acts, and coercive measures of all kinds, succeed, accompany, and overlap each other with melancholy persistence. The Union, according to its advocates, was to be the bond of lasting peace and affection between the two countries; it was followed by eighty-five years of coercive legislation. It is ironically appropriate that the Union so unlawfully accomplished could only be sustained by the complete abandonment of all ordinary processes of law thereafter.

The history of the recent movement may be told in a few words. At the general election of 1874 some sixty members were returned, under the leadership of Mr. Isaac Butt, as advocates of Home Rule, a term then just born into political life. Home Rule asks for Ireland a separate Government, still allied with the Imperial Government on the principle which regulates the relation of a State of the American Union with the central body at Washington. It became an active party under the leadership of Mr. Parnell after the general election of 1880. A land agitation, inaugurated by Mr. Michael Davitt, led to the foundation of the Land League, and famine, the League, and the Irish parliamentary party alike forced upon the Government the necessity of some fresh land legislation. The Government conceded legislation, suppressed the League, and did its best to suppress the parliamentary party. At one time Ireland was in the peculiar position of having almost all its leaders and most trusted representatives in prison at the same moment. When the Government at length set these leaders free and a new order of things seemed beginning, England and Ireland alike were horrified by the Invincible conspiracy, with its murder of Lord Frederick Cavendish and Mr. Burke—a conspiracy directly resulting from the extraordinary effort of the Government to stifle constitutional agitation in Ireland. A third general election has strikingly strengthened and intensified the Irish demand for self-government. Mr. Parnell has carried Ireland before him from the centre to the sea; he comes back to Westminster with a following of eighty-six members out of one hundred and three, and the political map of Ireland is almost entirely national, with the exception of a few seats in the far North which return Conservatives.

Thus far I have traced in briefest outline the main features of my country's history. It is the history of an undying love of liberty, of an unceasing protest against the unjust and unnatural imposition of a foreign creed, foreign laws, and foreign rulers. It is the history of a people who, in the face of almost unvarying calamity, have preserved their aspirations, reverenced their traditions, and persevered in their struggle for freedom with an unfaltering and unalterable patience and determination. I cannot but believe that the English people, examples of constitutional liberty themselves, champions of constitutional liberty in other countries, must sympathize with the Irishman's desire that he too should be constitutionally free, that he should govern and be governed after the manner most fitting to his race, his country, and his faith. If anything I have written can bring more clearly before the English mind Ireland's devotion through long centuries to her cause, and her passionate desire to dwell, as the other constituents of the Empire dwell, under the peaceful influence of laws drawn, like the blood of the pelican, from her own bosom for the use of her own offspring—if I can convince any Englishman that it is not merely just, but also profitable to end the quarrel of seven centuries, and have in Ireland an ally and not an enemy, I shall not have written in vain.

UNITED STATES CONSTITUTIONS.

By OAKEY HALL.

HOME RULE founded the United States of America one hundred and ten years ago. The Ministry of George the Third undertook to govern his colonies, in several material respects, from Westminster. The colonists then revolted and finally won their independence. Thirteen colonies became States, and together formed a confederacy. This soon led to republican union with a written Constitution, agreed to by the thirteen States which for all other purposes than dealing with Foreign Powers, managing the customs, the army, the navy, the postal service, the coinage, and the care of the territories not yet States, preserved their several autonomies of Home Rule, each within State borders. In self-defence against centralized oppression by the Congress, or Parliament of the Federal Union, the States provided a Supreme Federal Court, which had power to consider, on due case made, whether Federal statutes conformed to or disregarded the power surrendered by the States to the Central Government. It is a cardinal principle of American government that each State possesses every power and duty of government which are not expressly surrendered in the written Constitution to that Central Government by the various States. This Constitution cannot be modified or extended save by the voice of three-fourths of the States, now become by growth and progression of time thirty-eight in number. Of these, two were conquered from Mexico, besides a territory soon to become a State; one was purchased from France, another from Spain; and a territory—Alaska, some day to become a State—procured by treaty from Russia. The area of these States and territories begins at England's colony of New Brunswick, follows for an eastern boundary the Atlantic Ocean, takes the Gulf of Mexico for a southern boundary, and for a westward one the Mexican frontier, and in divergence the Pacific Ocean to the frontier of British America, thence over eastward to the place of beginning. The whole area of the United States and territories is nearly equal to four million square miles—within a million and a half of the area of the Chinese Empire, and within half the area of the Russian Empire. The territories number eleven. They are practically pure colonies, for they are mainly governed by the Federal or Central authority. Eight of them send delegates, locally elected, to the National or Federal Lower House. These delegates may debate, but have no votes. Some of the territories possess Legislatures, but with limited powers of local self-government. The territorial governors, principal rulers, and judges are appointed by the Federal authority. Twenty-four of the States have already been Federal territories. Probably all of the present territories will—unless jealousy from existing States prevent—become States within twenty years, and probably three within ten years. Territories are organized and controlled by Federal statutes. Within the past few months the Federal Legislature have passed Acts intended to utterly destroy polygamy practised by the Mormons in Utah Territory. Each State has a written Constitution, adopted—and from time to time capable of being amended—by a majority of the voters of the State at large. These Constitutions come from a similar democratic mould. Each one provides for a governor; a lieutenant-governor, who is presiding officer of the Senate or Upper House of Legislature, and possesses many *ex-officio* powers and duties: a Secretary of State, who cares for the records; one or more administrators of State taxes and finances; an attorney-general or law officer of State actions or prosecutions; and an official, variously named, who supervises canals, railways, and State public works. Each State has a Legislature of two Houses. The Lower House has a Speaker. Its members are universally paid, sometimes with a *per diem* (and travelling expenses), often by yearly salary. Each Legislature, by joint ballot at stated times and varying periods, selects two senators for the Federal Senate—the Upper House of the Federal Congress or Parliament. All of these State officers are chosen by popular suffrage. Thus, Federal senators are only once removed from the polls.

Federal representatives in the Lower House of Congress, or Federal Parliament, come directly from the people every two years. Each State, at stated periods, redistributes the area of the single districts from which each Congressman is elected. The number of districts and of the population entitled to send the member is according to Federal provision exclusively settled by the votes of all the State representatives or senators. Each State is divided by its constitution into counties, and each county into cities, towns, and villages, under State statutes. Every county has its own local Legislature, called by various names—sometimes Board of Supervisors, sometimes Board of Selectmen, often Board of Freeholders. This county Legislature is composed of delegates chosen by each town or municipal subdivision of county. It has certain defined powers of local legislation. Each county generally has its clerk, its public prosecutor, its Civil County Court, and general sessions of criminal jurisdiction; its recorder of deeds and mortgages, and its coroner and sanitary officers. Each town generally has a clerk, a justice of the peace, overseers of the poor, trustees of free public schools, poundmasters, and caretakers of bridges, roads, and highways. The legislature of each town consists of its adult inhabitants, who once a year assembled, commonly under presidency of a justice of the peace, in mass meeting, make enactments and governmental provisions, either by *viva voce* or by ballot. The Home Rule of each county or town is delegated to it by the State Legislature; but within the delegated powers or duties the county or town is locally supreme, subject only to writs of mandamus, certiorari, prohibition, or injunction, issued by the courts. Whenever cities exist within counties, these are governed, as in English cities, by a mayor, recorder, common councilmen, and their employés. Cities always, and generally towns, are made, for various purposes, incorporations. Universal suffrage is the general rule for Federal, State, or purely local government. The State of Rhode Island, which is in area precisely that of the county of Chester, forms the great exception. Property qualification and educational qualifications enter into the suffrage of a few States and of a large number of towns within States. The area of these States varies. We have just seen how small Rhode Island is; yet in protection of its State rights and its Home Rule relation to the Central Government it sends two senators to Washington, the capital of the nation; while its adjacent State of Massachusetts, that is seven times larger in area than Rhode Island, has only the same number of senators at Washington. One State (Texas) is twice as large in area as Great Britain and Ireland. The various State Constitutions contain some peculiar provisions. One, for instance, provides peculiar kinds of licences for the sale of intoxicating drinks. Two States absolutely prohibit such sale—a provision that is doubtful under the liberal spirit and letter of the Federal Constitution, which protects the freedom of contracts and of personal rights. One State (New York) forbids agricultural leases for more than twelve years of a term. Some Constitutions allow atheists to testify. All Constitutions secure the most absolute freedom of religious belief and practice, and forbid all tests, short of citizenship and convictions of felony, for the holding of place or office. All the Constitutions or State statutes prohibit primogeniture, devises beyond two lives, all feudal incidents of landholding or land transfers; stringently fetter trust estates and to a very large extent destroy distress for rent, and secure property of a homestead or work-for-a-living nature from seizure upon execution.

The great defect of State, or very local Home Rule in the various States, lies in conflict of law and ordinances. Each State has its own system of insolvency and of marriage or divorce, for instance; and often adjacent cities and towns have contentious ordinances. This situation very often produces social and commercial confusion; and our brief survey shows how extraordinarily extended and ramified is the system of Home Rule and local self-government in America. What may be called the drudgery of local government has been there transferred from central to local authority. Central or State, or municipal, or town, or village governments, as these exist in the United States, were well described by the late President Lincoln when he said, " Our Government is throughout one *of* the people *by* the people *for* the people." Moreover, the United States has no standing army. Its States-militia —governed entirely by local authority—constitutes the national defence, as the civil war proved. The Federal army existing to care only for territories, forts, and military posts along the unsettled frontiers, consisted, at a recent time of report upon its condition, of only 2,147 officers and 24,236 enlisted men. All police authority and police creation spring exclusively from local authority throughout the thirty-eight States. Indeed, so thoroughly under the Federal and State Constitutions of the United States is heard *vox populi*, that if any criticism is to be made upon local government therein, the point might arise for discussion, that there exists too much independence, too much Home Rule, and a superfluity of local self-government in the republic that conquered its nationality from Great Britain.

THE CONSTITUTION OF SWITZERLAND.

BY DR. WILLIAM BURCKHARDT.

THE Swiss Republic was formerly a confederation of independent Governments, and had up to modern times no central legislative and administrative bodies. An assembly of official representatives from the Cantons "Diète," voting according to instructions from their respective Goverments, had the following principal functions: treaties with Foreign Powers; declaration of war and peace; maintenance of friendly relations (including arbitration of conflicts) between the cantons, &c. A change was made, in consequence of the French Revolution, at the end of the last century; but only the Constitution of 1848 created central authorities, with the power to deal exclusively with a vast sphere of legislative subjects.

The present Federal Constitution, dated May 29, 1874, accentuated still further this centralistic tendency.

A. *Federal Legislative Bodies.*

The Federal Chambers are—

1. The National Council ("Conseil National"), elected by the whole body of voters for three years. Every male Swiss over twenty years has a vote, the cantons retaining the right to disable bankrupts, paupers, lunatics. One representative for every 20,000 inhabitants (or fractions over 10,000). Election districts of various sizes, returning

one to five representatives. A redistribution on a fair basis of equality (single member constituencies) is desired by a large section of the people. Present number of representatives, 145.

2. The States Council ("Conseil des Etats"), 44 members; two for each of the cantons. This second Chamber is a concession to the old "federative" principle; the cantons having formerly possessed equality of rights, it has been thought wise to give the same number of representatives to the smallest (Zug, with 92 sq. miles and 23,000 inhabitants), as well as to the largest canton (Berne, with 2,660 sq. miles and 532,000 inhabitants).

Laws must pass both Chambers (by absolute majorities). There is no provision against a conflict between the Houses, but collisions are very rare.

Either 30,000 voters or eight cantons have the right to ask, by written declaration, for the submission of any new law to the vote of the general body of electors. This is called "Referendum," and has only been introduced in 1874. The clause has proved already a practical one.

B. *Federal Executive Body* (" *Conseil Fédéral*").

Seven members, elected for three years by the two Chambers united in Congress. The President of the Confederation (and of this Council) is elected for one year.

This Federal Council has the following principal functions:—
1. Relations with Foreign Powers.
2. Supervision of execution of laws.
3. Guarantee of " rights of citizens."
4. Drafting of laws for the Chambers.
5. Provisional mobilizing of army.
6. Control of federal administration.

C. *Sphere of Federal Laws and Prerogatives.*

Supreme principle of the division of the legislative and administrative powers between federal and cantonal authorities is still the following :—Cantons are considered independent, "souverains," in all matters not expressly reserved by the Federal Constitution to the central authorities.

In virtue of the Constitution, the Confederation exercises the following privileges, to the absolute exclusion of the cantons :—

1. War and peace. 2. Treaties with other Powers. 3. Army. 4. Customs. 5. Post and telegraphs. 6. Coinage. 7. Manufacture of powder.

Laws concerning these matters are drawn up exclusively by the Federal Chambers, as likewise those on the following subjects :—

1. Certain parts of the civil law (commercial law, law of contracts). 2. Parts of criminal law (treason, &c.). 3. Matrimony. 4. Registration of births, deaths, and marriages. 5. Hunting and fishing. 6. Bank-notes. 7. Weights and measures. 8. Construction of railways. 9. Factory laws. 10. Naturalization of foreigners. 11. Emigration (supervision of).

Moreover, the Federal Constitution has guaranteed the inviolability of the following principles, which are not to be overruled by cantonal laws :—

1. Equality of all citizens before the law.
2. Liberty of commerce and of trades (excepting salt, powder, alcoholic drinks).
3. Faculty to choose a domicile in any part of Switzerland.
4. Liberty of creed and conscience.

THE CONSTITUTION OF SWITZERLAND. 159

5. Liberty of holding religious services, if compatible with public order and decency.
6. Liberty of Press and of associations.
7. Right of free education in primary schools.

D. *The Cantons.*

The Swiss Republic consists of the following 22 cantons in historic order :—

Zürich	square miles	665	inhabitants	317,576
Bern	,,	2,660	,,	523,164
Luzern	,,	580	,,	134,806
Uri	,,	415	,,	23,694
Schwyz	,,	351	,,	51,235
Unterwalden	,,	295	,,	27,348
Glarus	,,	267	,,	34,213
Zug	,,	92	,,	22,994
Freiberg	,,	644	,,	115,400
Solothurn	,,	303	,,	80,424
Basel	,,	177	,,	124,372
Schafthausen	,,	116	,,	38,348
Appenzell	,,	162	,,	66,799
St. Gallen	,,	780	,,	210,401
Graubünden	,,	2,774	,,	94,991
Aargau	,,	542	,,	198,645
Thurgan	,,	382	,,	99,552
Ticino	,,	1,095	,,	130,777
Vaud	,,	1,245	,,	238,730
Valais	,,	2,026	,,	100,216
Neuchâtel	,,	312	,,	103,732
Genéve	,,	109	,,	101,595

Some of the cantons are vesting the legislative power in

the "Landsgemeinde"—*i.e.*, the whole body of adult citizens, assembled on certain days for the purpose of deliberating in open-air meetings on the proposed laws; but most of the cantons have a legislative Chamber, called "Great Council," elected by all voters (same franchise as for federal votes). In almost all of these Cantons the electors cooperate with the Great Councils, possessing either the "facultative" or the "obligatory" referendum.

The cantons have their own constitutions, which must be approved by the federal authorities, and are vetoed if containing anything opposed to the principle contained in the Federal Constitution.

The cantons deal independently with the following matters (besides subjects of minor importance):—1. Education. 2. Taxation. 3. Criminal law. 4. Civil law (with exceptions mentioned above). 5. Tribunals (there being, however, a Federal Tribunal as Court of Supreme Appeal. 6. Police. 7. National churches. 8. Public works. 9. Communal administration. 10. Pauperism.

THE DUAL SYSTEM OF GOVERNMENT OF HUNGARY AND AUSTRIA.

By Dr. F. L. WEINMANN.

DURING the recent discussion of the question of Home Rule for Ireland in the newspapers, reference has repeatedly been made to the position of Hungary in her political and constitutional relations to Austria as an example that might with advantage be applied to Ireland in order to satisfy her demand for self-government.

Although there are certain points of similarity in the relative positions of Hungary towards Austria and Ireland to Great Britain, yet in many other and very important respects there is as wide a difference between the two countries as possibly can be.

As in some other countries, so in Austria, the first germs of Constitutionalism may be traced many centuries back, and though no such solid foundation-stone can be pointed to as the glorious Magna Charta of which the English are so justly proud, already in mediæval ages the creation of consultative and deliberative assemblies had been effected, with the view of achieving political unity, and thereby the several classes of the State were led into a more or less direct participation in the work of government. The earliest Austrian representative bodies, or Diets, consisted of the so-called four Estates—the Prelates, the Barons, the Knights, and the Citizens. Their origin dates very far back, and from the time of the Emperor Maximilian's death, in 1519, up to the reign of Joseph II., a sort of "Reichsrath," or Imperial Council, more or less complete, is continually recurring, and has, with many modifications and long interruptions, endured to our days.

The chief aim the Government had then in view was to a certain degree the same as now—namely, unity of administration, or rather co-operation of each separate part of the monarchy with the other parts of it, so as to arrive at a just distribution of general political rights and duties without encroaching upon the particular privileges of each nationality.

Joseph II. shelved all representative institutions; but Leopold II., immediately after his accession, convoked the Diets of every province, in order to enable them to submit their grievances and wishes to him. In the first Diet of 1790 the cities were represented; the following year, however, they were excluded; and henceforth it became customary to invite the Fourth Estate to be present only at the reading of financial reports, and to record their vote to edicts of taxation in writing.

Whilst the Estates of the so-called hereditary Austrian provinces sank by degrees into insignificance, the Hungarian Constitution, though far from being a model Constitution, or in any way in accordance with the principles of modern constitutional life, remained in all force, and was recognized by Joseph II. when he revoked, shortly before his death, all the measures decreed during his reign against the free exercise of it. Its validity was acknowledged until the year 1848, and though its abrogation was greatly regretted at the time by all the Hungarian patriots, their new Constitution, voted in that year, which was long in abeyance, was ultimately recognized by the Emperor's sanction on February 17, 1867, and now forms the foundation of Hungary's political independence. But severe and long was the struggle until the Hungarians had achieved this point. Indeed, it was not until the end of that eventful year 1866, during which Austria, after her defeat in the battles of Königgrätz and Sadowa, was deprived of her influence and position in Germany, and relieved of that great burden and standing source of weakness, the possession of Venice, that Hungary—thanks to the wise and indefatigable exertions of Baron von Beust, the Austrian Minister for Foreign Affairs at that time, in which he was most ably and energetically assisted by that distinguished Hungarian patriot, Francis Deák, the leader of the moderate Hungarian Liberals—at last, after a struggle of nineteen years, stood upon the threshold of the fulfilment of her wishes.

In an address drawn up by Francis Deák, the Hungarian Diet, which had been prorogued on account of the war, put into a precise form the position and the demands of Hungary for the re-establishment of a parliamentary and legal municipal Government. Hungary, it was stated, required a real constitutional rule, the establishment of which was by no means a political impossibility. By a rescript of the Emperor, dated the 17th of November, and addressed to the Hungarian Diet, his Majesty replied, that in resuming the thread of negotiations with the Diet, on the basis of the terms mentioned in the Speech from the Throne, the principal object to be accomplished was the constitutional settlement of the connection of the different parts of the monarchy, and the speedy re-establishment of the autonomous rights of Hungary. The Emperor regretted the prorogation of the Diet just at the time when the sub-committee of the Commission of 67 members had drawn up their report with reference to the discussion and the treatment of the common or imperial affairs, which his Majesty recognized as a fitting basis for the establishment of a constitutional settlement. The rescript also indicated the several points in regard to which it appeared requisite that the special attention of the Estates and the representatives should be directed. These were: firstly, the maintenance of the unity of the army with unity of command, its organization, and also the rules regulating the terms of service and recruitment; secondly, the regulation, according to uniform principles, of the customs, of the indirect taxation, of the State monopoly system, and of the public debt and State credit. "If," continued the rescript, "the deliberations of the Diet result in removing the obstacles connected with the unity of the monarchy, which must be upheld, then the constitutional wishes and demands of Hungary, put forward in the address of the Diet, will be fulfilled by the appointment of a responsible Ministry, and by the restoration of the municipal autonomy. The system of the responsibility of the Government will be introduced, not only in Hungary, but in all parts of the monarchy. The detailed application and realization of the principles referring to the common affairs, as well as to the modifications to be introduced in the laws of 1848, will be carried out by responsible Ministers, to be appointed in agreement with the Estates and representatives in Diet assembled."

Shortly before Christmas, on the 20th of December 1866, Baron von Beust, accompanied by the Hungarian Court Chancellor, paid a visit to Pesth, in order to confer with the leading men of the country, and hold out the olive branch to that uneasy and dissatisfied kingdom, the Cabinet of Vienna having come to the conclusion to make the Hungarians all concessions compatible with the unity of the empire and the duty of the Government towards all the other nationalities of the monarchy.

Being a conglomeration of different countries and different nationalities, it was no small task to give each country the proper Constitution, and then to mould the various elements into such a form as to make the governmental machine perform its work in a satisfactory and beneficial manner; but Baron von Beust's negotiations at Pesth were attended with decided success. His programme was based on the principle of the autonomy of Hungary and the endowment of all the other countries of the empire with an equal amount of liberty and autonomy.

On the 6th of February the Committee concluded their labours on the common affairs, and their report was to form the basis of the settlement of the pending differences between the Crown and the kingdom of Hungary. On the 18th of the same month an imperial rescript was read in both Houses of the Hungarian Diet, announcing that the Emperor assented to the demands embodied in the Diet's address of the 17th of January relative to the decree for the reorganization of the army. The Emperor at the same time, confiding in the loyalty of the Hungarian nation, and putting entire faith in her readiness to co-operate with him to preserve the empire, restored the Hungarian Constitution, charging Count Julius Andrássy with the formation of a responsible Ministry; thus constituting the empire on the dualistic principle. He professed to desire the integrity of Hungary, and promised to defend the Constitution; but hoped and expected that all the people would defend the throne and the empire, that the Diet would fulfil the terms of the arrangement as promised in its address, would carry out the object of the Pragmatic Sanction, and grant an indemnity to the Ministry.

It was a proud moment for the patriotic statesman when Count Andrássy, on the 24th of February, announced to the Diet his appointment as President of the Ministry, submitting at the same time the list of his colleagues, who, without passion or resentment, had with him steadily pursued the path of constitutional legality, had reconciled the kingdom with the Crown, and restored it to its old place in the

Austrian State system. It was also a triumph for Baron von Beust, the first Austrian statesman who had had the courage and resolution to carry the most urgent but long-delayed settlement to a satisfactory conclusion. Hungary was reconciled ; her ardently cherished aspirations were realized ; the discord which had so long subsisted between the Emperor and his Hungarian subjects, and which was disastrous alike for Austria and for Hungary, threatening the whole State with dissolution, was brought to a close ; and the solemn coronation of Francis Joseph at Pesth, with the crown of St. Stephen, on the 8th of June 1867, symbolized the final restoration of peace with the Hungarian people. Hungary has since that date had a national representation based on the most liberal law of election ; she has a Ministry dependent on parliamentary control ; a Constitution with the highest constitutional guarantees, and the solemn oath of her Sovereign to preserve that Constitution ; she has the undivided rule of her national Government over the entire territory of the crown of St. Stephen, the fullest measure of religious freedom, and an army of her own.

There remains now only to summarize briefly the various laws enacted on the basis of the settlement concluded, in accordance with the terms of the report of the special Parliamentary Commission. They are seven in number : —

1. The law of 12th June 1867, for the regulation of the affairs regarded as common to the whole empire.

2. The law of 27th December 1867, respecting the proportionate share to be contributed by Hungary, according to the preceding law, towards the expenditure of the common or imperial affairs.

3. The laws of 24th December 1867 and 27th December 1867, by which the share to be contributed annually from the Hungarian revenues towards the liquidation of the common State debt is regulated.

4. The laws of 27th December 1867 and 27th June 1878, respectively, relating to the conclusion of a commercial and customs union between Hungary, as an independent constitutional State, and the Austrian portions of the monarchy.

I. Imperial affairs, or affairs regarded as common between countries of Austria proper and the countries of the Hungarian crown, are the following :—

1. All *foreign affairs*, including the diplomatic and commercial representation of the empire in foreign countries, and all measures rendered necessary by virtue of international treaties, reserving, however, the constitutional sanction of such international treaties, in so far as such should be required, to the Legislatures of the two portions of the monarchy, the Austrian Reichsrath at Vienna and the Hungarian Reichstag at Pesth.

2. All *military affairs*, including those of the imperial navy, excepting, however, the legislative authorization for the levying of recruits, and the legislative enactments relating to the military service in general, and the distribution and quartering as well as the maintenance of the troops; also the regulation of the civil rights of the soldiery, and all matters concerning the duties and obligations of the troops not strictly appertaining to military service and discipline.

3. All matters of *imperial finance* having reference to the common expenditure, and in particular the legislative approval of the respective budgets and the audit of the accounts.

The following, though not subject to common administration, shall be treated according to uniform principles periodically to be agreed upon :—

1. All commercial affairs, and in particular the legislation as to customs duties and imposts to be levied.

2. Legislation with reference to the indirect taxation in regard to manufactures and industrial productions.

3. The regulation of the money standard and coinage.

4. The regulations required in respect of those railway lines which affect the interests of both halves of the monarchy.

5. The organization of the system of defence.

The expenditure required for the administration of common affairs is to be shared in proportion by the two halves of the monarchy, as may be determined by common agreement of the two Legislatures, with the sanction of the monarch.

In case no agreement should be arrived at by the two Legislatures, the proportionate share to be contributed by each half of the monarchy will be fixed by the Emperor, but only for one year. The provision for the proportionate contribution is, however, a matter to be dealt with by the respective Legislatures.

In regard to loans rendered necessary in behalf of the expenditure for common—*i.e.*, imperial—affairs, the conditions as well as the terms of repayment, and the disbursement of the same, must be treated in the same manner as other imperial affairs.

The administration of common or imperial affairs will be placed in the hands of a responsible common Ministry, which, however, is prohibited from conducting any of the separate affairs of government of one or the other of the two halves of the monarchy, in conjunction with their ministerial functions as to the administration of the imperial affairs.

All measures, ordinances, &c., concerning the command and the organization of the army are the exclusive prerogative of the Sovereign.

The right of legislation appertaining to the Legislatures

of both halves of the monarchy will be exercised by a separate parliamentary body—the Delegations—composed of sixty members (of whom one-third are to be elected by simple majority from among the members of the Upper House, and the other two-thirds from among the deputies of the House of Representatives) from each Legislature of the two portions of the monarchy. Substitutes for absentees, or vacancies occurring, will be elected by each of the two Houses of the Austrian and the Hungarian Central Diets, in the proportion of ten of the Upper House to twenty of the Lower House. The election of Delegates and substitutes takes place annually at the commencement of each session. Previous members may be re-elected.

The Delegations are summoned annually by the Emperor to meet in special session alternately at Vienna and at Pesth. They elect each their own president, vice-president, secretaries, and other officials required.

To the competence of the Delegations belong chiefly all matters concerning the imperial affairs of the empire. All other matters are excluded from their constitutional functions. All bills, motions, &c., must be submitted to each Delegation separately by the common Ministry.

All laws to be passed on matters within the competence of both Delegations require the unanimous concurrence of both the Delegations; and in case of no unanimity being achievable, the assent of a majority of the votes taken in a division of a joint meeting of both Delegations is necessary, subject in each case to the sanction of the Emperor.

The right of impeachment of the common Ministry is vested in both the Delegations.

At least thirty members of each Delegation must be present to form a quorum, and all motions and resolutions must be passed by an absolute majority of votes. Voting by proxy is not permitted. Retirement from the Reichsrath or Reichstag implies retirement likewise from the membership of the respective Delegations. With the dissolution of either the Austrian Reichsrath or the Hungarian Reichstag the functions of the Delegations cease also. The new Reichsrath or Reichstag elects at its meeting a fresh Delegation each.

The sittings of the Delegations are open to the public. Each Delegation is entitled to demand that, in case of a divergence of opinion, the question under consideration shall be decided by a joint vote; two-thirds at least of the members of each Delegation being required to be present at such joint meeting to form a quorum. The decision is carried by the absolute majority of the votes at the division.

II. By the laws of 27th December 1867 and 27th June 1878, the proportionate amount to be contributed annually from the Austrian and the Hungarian State Treasury respectively towards the common expenditure of the monarchy has been fixed by mutual legislative agreement at seventy per cent. for the Austrian portion of the monarchy, and at thirty per cent. for the countries of the Hungarian crown; but when subsequently the military frontier was incorporated with Hungary, the proportions were amended to 68·6 for Austria, and Hungary 31·4 per cent. Hungary having an equal representation with Austria in the management of their common affairs, this arrangement would seem to give an undue advantage to Hungary over Austria, but in practice it has, on the whole, worked well.

This proportion of the respective contributions shall remain unalterably in force for a period of ten years from January 1, 1866, till December 31, 1877, and December 31, 1887, respectively; to be renewed hereafter, by common agreement, periodically, from ten to ten years.

By sect. 64 of the law of 12th June 1867 it has been provided that the net amount of revenue derived from the customs duties, as an imperial source of State income, shall above all things be applied towards the defrayment of the common expenditure; but with this limitation, that from this net amount of customs revenues all drawbacks on account of duties paid at the custom-houses on export goods shall first be deducted, and the balance devoted to the reduction of the gross amount of the common expenditure, which is to be lessened approximately by that amount in the budget estimates.

III. By the laws of the 24th and 27th December 1867 it was enacted that, commencing from January 1, 1868, the countries of the Hungarian Crown shall have to contribute, unalterably and irrevocably, towards the redemption and the charges of the Imperial State debt, the sum of 29,188,000 florins, including 11,776,000 florins to be paid in specie.

The floating debt, consisting of notes and other paper currency, amounting at that time altogether to 312 million florins, was by that law placed under the joint guarantee of both divisions of the monarchy.

A special Liquidation Commission was appointed for the examination and adjustment of all the assets of the central (imperial) finances, which, with the exclusion of the arrears of the taxes to which each part of the monarchy is proportionately entitled, were designed for the payment of the interest and capital of the public debt due up to the last day of December 1867. Both the Treasury of the countries of the Hungarian Crown and that of the western division of Austria are bound to transmit every month to the common imperial exchequer, as is the case in respect of their contributions towards the expenditure of the administration of the common affairs of the empire, a certain portion of their monthly revenues on account of their contribution towards the redemption, including the payment of the interest of the national debt, which monthly remittances must be of the same amount, in proportion to the monthly receipts, as the sum total of the contributions compared with the gross amount of the budget estimates of the expenditure of each current year.

IV. In accordance with the laws of 27th December 1867 and 27th June 1878, respectively, in regard to the commercial and customs union established between the countries of the Hungarian Crown and the Austrian portions of the monarchy, the whole territory of both divisions of the empire constitutes, for the purpose of the management of all commercial matters, customs, and navigation affairs, during the whole term this agreement is in force, one entire State, circumscribed by one common customs boundary.

Consequently, neither of the two divisions of the monarchy will have the right during this time to impose upon articles of trade or manufacture which are being transmitted from any of the different countries of the one half of the empire to those of the other half, and *vice versa*, any kind of imposts—import, export, or transition duties—or any tolls or taxes whatsoever, or to establish for this purpose any intermediate customs boundary.

Either division of the empire is permitted to charge any inland duties of whatever description—no matter for whomsoever levied—upon articles of commerce imported from any parts of the other division, only so far and to such an extent as the similar native industrial and commercial products or manufactures of its own division are burdened with home duties in any of the various countries within its own territory.

The treaties concluded with foreign States for the regulation of the international commercial and economical relations, such as treaties of commerce, customs conventions, navigation treaties, consular, post, and telegraph conventions, are considered equally binding for the various countries of the two divisions of the empire.

The negotiation and conclusion of treaties or conventions of a similar character by the Minister for Foreign Affairs can in future, however, only be effected subject to the assent of the constitutional factors of the empire—the Austrian and Hungarian central Parliaments—and the concurrence of the special Ministers of the two halves of the empire.

The collection and administration of the customs revenues are reserved exclusively to the respective Governments of the two divisions of the empire within the limits of their particular territory.

The control of all matters connected with the management of ports and harbours and maritime sanitary affairs and sea navigation, including sea fisheries, will be exercised by the respective Governments of the two divisions of the country separately, but according to uniform rules and conform principles.

All matters having reference to the protection of sea-trading vessels and their crews, and the protection of the sailors and their interests in foreign countries, belong to the jurisdiction of the imperial and royal consulates in those countries, and the common Minister for Foreign Affairs.

All shipping and other navigation dues and charges, the collection and administration of which must take place according to uniform rules and regulations, belong to the Government of the country in which they have been collected.

The same rules apply to all local taxation, and such indirect taxes as directly affect articles of consumption, such as the excise duties on beer, alcoholic drinks, sugar, &c.

The existing monetary system of Austrian currency, as well as the metrical system of weights and measures, shall remain in force.

There shall be perfectly free intercourse and equality, without let or hindrance, in respect of all trade, commerce, and occupation, and the exercise of one's profession or business, &c., between the inhabitants of all countries of the two territorial divisions constituting the empire.

The same principles of parity apply to all patents of inventions, protection of trade-marks, &c., hitherto granted and henceforth to be granted in accordance with the existing laws, which shall be valid equally in the countries of both divisions of the monarchy.

The administration of the post and telegraph service, organized and regulated on general uniform principles, is a matter solely under the control of the respective home Governments.

This commercial and customs union shall remain in force from the 1st July 1878 till 31st December 1887, and at the expiration of that term continued or be renewed periodically every ten years.

The concluding law of the series, regulating the political and other relations between Hungary and Austria, which emanated from the settlement of 1867, is the law of the 17th of November 1868, by which the convention concluded in reference to the settlement of the political and constitutional relations between Hungary and Croatia, Slavonia and Dalmatia, was sanctioned, which countries henceforth form, on the basis of the Pragmatic Sanction, or fundamental charter of the Emperor Charles VI. of 1720, of the Dual Empire, *one united State community*, as well in relation to the other individual States under the dominion of his Majesty as in relation to foreign countries.

These countries enjoy, as integral parts of the countries of the Crown of St. Stephen, in administrative and legislative respects and executive power, the same consitutional independence and autonomy as Hungary, and are represented in the Hungarian Ministerial Council by a separate Minister without portfolio. They also send, in proportion to the number of their population, twenty-nine deputies (two of them to the Upper House) to the United Reichstag or Central Parliament at Pesth, of which number five (four elected by the Lower House and one on the part of the Upper House) are delegated to represent the Croatian and Slavonian Diets in the session of the Delegations.

At the head of the autonomous Croatian, Slavonian, and Dalmatian Governments is the " Banus " (a dignity answering to the position of provincial or colonial governor), vested with civil authority only, who is appointed by the Emperor-King, with the counter-signature of the Hungarian Prime Minister, but who is responsible for his official acts to the Croatian and Slavonian Diet.

Such is in brief the substance of the various enactments by virtue of which the dual *régime* in Hungary and Austria was established. What an important gain has accrued to the Imperial Austrian State from the compromise effected with Hungary twenty years ago can only be justly estimated by those who recall to mind the bitter animosity which existed for so many years between Hungary and Austria, and the incessant dissensions and protests, accompanied by a stubborn, passive resistance, and the general refusal to pay the taxes levied by the unconstitutional Austrian Government which had not been sanctioned by the Hungarian Diet, and all the ill-success and the disasters suffered by Austria, which chiefly resulted from this calamitous state of affairs, particularly in connection with the wars with Italy, France, and Prussia.

The advantages obtained from having silenced the opposition and removed the causes of the passive resistance of the Hungarian people, by the fulfilment of their aspirations and wishes, have subdued and calmed the scruples of those who apprehended from these concessions, which they regarded as excessive and too far-reaching, nothing but a disintegrating danger to the integrity and union of the empire.

The results have proved that the dangers of a system of free and liberal dualism are far less than a state of continuous discontent and internal war and lawlessness with a nation which is only reluctantly and sullenly bowing its neck under the iron rule of its fancied oppressors, and that the scheme of converting that nation by liberal concessions into an active and useful co-partner in a new order of things was not only a happy and correct one, but also one of beneficial success, provided that this nation was, besides its proved inflexibility and perseverance, possessed of a sufficiently high degree of self-restraint and self-abnegation to subordinate, by a moderate and wise use and application of the concessions obtained and the success achieved thereby, their own interests to the higher and imperial interests and the well-being of the whole State.

"There can be no doubt that the dual *régime* has acted beneficially as regards Hungary," since, according to one of her own highest authorities, the present condition of that country is in harmony with the real wants of the nation, the different political parties standing on the firm foundation of loyalty to the Crown, a circumstance which affords a sufficient guarantee for the future of the Hungarian State and the indissoluble union of the empire.

STATISTICAL TABLES.

PREPARED BY

W. LEIGH BERNARD,

*Barrister-at-law; Fellow of the Statistical Society of London; Editor of
"Leading Cases decided under 'The Irish Church Acts,' &c."*

POPULATION OF THE UNITED KINGDOM

From 1700 to 1881 (partly estimated).

Year	ENGLAND AND WALES. (Total area, 37,319,221 statute acres.)	SCOTLAND. (Total area, 19,496,132 statute acres.)	IRELAND. (Total area, 20,819,829 statute acres.)	TOTAL UNITED KINGDOM. (Total area, 77,635,182 statute acres.)	Year.
1700	5,400,000	1,000,000	1,375,000	7,775,000	1700
1750	6,950,000	1,225,000	2,365,000	10,540,000	1750
1790	8,545,000	1,510,000	4,150,000	14,205,000	1790
1801	8,892,536	1,608,420	5,300,000	15,800,956	1801
1811	10,164,256	1,805,864	5,700,000	17,670,120	1811
1821	12,000,236	2,091,521	6,801,827	20,893,584	1821
1831	13,896,797	2,364,386	7,767,401	24,028,584	1831
1841	15,906,741	2,620,184	8,175,124	26,702,049	1841
1851	17,927,609	2,888,742	6,574,278	27,390,629	1851
1861	20,066,224	3,062,294	5,798,967	28,927,485	1861
1871	22,712,266	3,360,018	5,412,377	31,484,661	1871
1881	25,974,439	3,735,573	5,174,836	34,884,848	1881

POPULATION OF BRITISH EMPIRE.—The population of the British Empire at the Census of 1881 was 254,187,630, including 207,462,389 in Asia, 4,520,415 in North America, 2,914,176 in Australasia, 2,579,163 in Africa, 1,243,861 in the West Indies and Central America, 327,805 in Europe, and 254,532 in South America.

IRELAND.

RELIGIOUS PROFESSIONS, UNITED KINGDOM, 1881.

The Census of England and Scotland does not contain particulars of the Religious Professions of the people. It has been estimated that the members of the Established Church in England number about 14,000,000, and the Roman Catholics in Great Britain about 2,000,000. In Ireland the Census returns of 1881 show that the Roman Catholics numbered 3,960,891, or 76·6 per cent. of population; the members of the Disestablished Church, 639,574, or 12·4 per cent.; the Presbyterians, 470,734, or 9·0 per cent.; Methodists, 48,839; Independents, 6,210; Baptists, 4,879; Society of Friends, 3,645; and Jews, 472.

RELIGIOUS DIVISIONS OF THE WORLD.

Estimate from Schem's Statistics of the World in the " American Almanac."

Continent.	Roman Catholics.	Protestants.	Eastern Churches.	Total Population.
Europe . .	147,300,000	71,500,000	69,300,000	301,800,000
America .	*47,300,000	30,000,000	......	84,500,000
Asia . .	4,900,000	1,800,000	8,500,000	798,000,000
Africa . .	1,100,000	1,200,000	3,200,000	203,300,000
Australasia .	400,000	1,500,000	......	4,400,000
Total .	201,000,000	106,000,000	81,000,000	1,392,000,000

* Including about 7,000,000 resident in the United States.

```
Total Christian population   .   .   .   .   388,000,000
Buddhists   .   .   .   .   .   .   .   340,000,000
Mohammedans   .   .   .   .   .   .   201,000,000
Brahmanism   .   .   .   .   .   .   175,000,000
Followers of Confucius   .   .   .   .   80,000,000
Sinto Religion   .   .   .   .   .   .   14,000,000
Judaism   .   .   .   .   .   .   .    7,000,000
Heathens   .   .   .   .   .   .   .   187,000,000
```

NATIVES OF SCOTLAND, IRELAND, AND OTHER PARTS,

Resident in England and Wales at each of the last five Censuses.

	PERSONS.				
	1841.	1851.	1861.	1871.	1881.
Total enumerated Population	15,906,741	17,927,609	20,066,224	22,712,266	25,974,439
Born in England and Wales	15,441,530	17,165,656	19,120,052	21,692,165	24,855,822
„ other Parts	465,211	761,953	946,172	1,020,101	1,118,617
„ Scotland	103,768	130,087	169,202	213,254	253,528
„ Ireland	290,891	519,959	601,634	566,540	562,374
„ Islands in the British Seas	11,705	13,753	18,423	25,655	29,316
„ Colonies and India	17,248	33,688	51,572	70,812	94,399
„ Foreign Parts	39,446	61,708	101,832	139,445	174,372
„ Ships at Sea	2,153	2,758	3,509	4,395	4,628

NOTE.—The numbers in the column for 1841, in the above Table, given as "born in Islands in the British Seas, Colonies, and India, and in Ships at Sea," were calculated from the corresponding numbers in 1851, 1861, and 1871; and 81,237, "not specified where born," have been distributed proportionally throughout the column.

180   IRELAND.

ARMY.—Average Strength of the British Army in England, Scotland, Ireland, and Abroad, in each year from 1865 to 1884, distinguishing the number of Officers and Men.

Year	Officers: England and Wales	Officers: Scotland	Officers: Ireland	Officers: Total at Home	Officers: Abroad	Officers: Total Officers	Warrant Officers: England and Wales	Warrant Officers: Scotland	Warrant Officers: Ireland	Warrant Officers: Total at Home	Warrant Officers: Abroad	Warrant Officers: Total Warrant Officers	Non-Commissioned Officers and Men: England and Wales	Non-Commissioned Officers and Men: Scotland	Non-Commissioned Officers and Men: Ireland	Non-Commissioned Officers and Men: Total at Home	Non-Commissioned Officers and Men: Abroad	Non-Commissioned Officers and Men: Total Non-Commissioned Officers and Men	General Total
1865	3,198	185	1,074	4,457	6,372	10,829							56,584	3,444	20,017	80,045	118,003	198,048	208,877
1866	3,021	180	1,269	4,470	6,252	10,722							53,456	3,229	22,969	79,654	111,265	190,919	201,641
1867	3,094	173	1,209	4,476	6,078	10,554							57,250	3,344	22,537	83,131	106,650	189,781	200,335
1868	3,345	214	1,095	4,654	5,738	10,392							60,595	3,922	20,462	84,979	101,529	186,508	196,900
1869	3,422	181	1,133	4,736	5,473	10,209							58,089	3,108	20,345	81,542	94,917	176,459	186,668
1870	3,352	192	1,278	4,822	4,805	9,627							58,024	3,278	23,546	84,848	85,969	170,817	180,444
1871	3,495	169	1,216	4,880	4,314	9,194							71,147	3,293	26,437	100,877	82,594	183,471	192,665
1872	3,480	171	1,197	4,848	4,144	8,992							69,994	3,298	26,014	99,306	83,709	183,015	192,007
1873	3,487	207	1,121	4,815	3,877	8,692							67,637	3,741	24,390	95,768	83,919	179,687	188,379
1874	3,317	208	996	4,521	3,763	8,284							67,577	4,000	21,537	93,114	84,991	178,105	186,389
1875	3,171	218	1,002	4,391	3,691	8,082							66,308	3,955	22,539	92,802	83,785	176,587	184,669
1876	3,156	213	996	4,365	3,776	8,141							67,201	3,824	21,751	92,781	83,511	176,292	184,433
1877	3,122	209	963	4,294	3,766	8,060							72,185	3,674	21,756	97,610	84,832	182,442	190,502
1878	3,105	196	894	4,195	3,750	7,945							77,495	4,437	23,074	105,006	87,807	192,813	*200,758
1879	2,881	163	791	3,835	4,007	7,842							62,633	3,854	17,893	84,380	99,068	183,448	191,290
1880	2,989	186	869	4,044	3,773	7,817	291	18	93	402	209	611	58,908	3,820	19,715	87,843	93,326	181,169	188,986
1881	2,722	180	1,052	3,954	3,658	7,612	290	16	91	397	214	611	58,909	3,610	25,473	87,992	93,194	181,186	188,798
1882	2,568	146	1,114	3,818	3,518	7,336							58,466	3,445	28,164	90,075	91,207	181,282	188,798
1883	2,550	135	1,029	3,714	3,479	7,193							59,281	3,185	23,494	85,960	88,207	174,167	181,971
1884	2,473	134	971	3,578	3,519	7,097	293	16	94	403	220	623	59,399	3,250	23,364	86,013	89,271	175,284	183,004

N.B.—Regiments on passage out and home are included with the numbers "ABROAD."

* The increase in the average strength of the Army during this year is due to the Mobilization of the First-class Army and Militia Reserves during three months of the period.

STATISTICAL TABLES.

ARMY.—*Nationalities of the Non-Commissioned Officers and Men on the 1st January 1885.*

Corps of Army Service.	English.	Scotch.	Irish.	Born in India or the Colonies.	Foreigners.	Not reported.	Total.
Household Cavalry	973	178	86	16	...	..	1,253
Cavalry of the Line	12,325	1,168	1,492	170	4	60	15,219
Royal Artillery	22,546	2,024	5,201	713	50	83	30,617
Royal Engineers	3,813	347	528	119	8	...	4,815
Foot Guards	4,861	767	344	13	5	2	5,992
Infantry of the Line	78,912	8,938	22,902	1,159	78	3,361	115,350
Colonial Corps	24	4	7	2,142	1	21	2,199
Commissariat and Transport Corps	2,289	141	280	43	4	...	2,757
Ordnance Store Corps	458	45	63	16	1	...	583
Corps of Ordnance Artificers	29	1	3	...	...	...	33
Medical Staff Corps	1,815	111	234	23	7	...	2,190
General total	128,045	13,724	31,140	4,414	158	3,527	181,008
Proportion per 1000	730	78	178	13	1	...	1,000

ARMY.—*Religious Denominations of the Non-Commissioned Officers and Men on the 1st January 1885.*

Corps of Army Service.	Church of England.	Presbyterians.	Wesleyans.	Other Protestants.	Roman Catholics.	Mahommedans, Hindoos, Jews, &c.	Not reported.	Total.
Household Cavalry	1,080	120	6	...	47	...	...	1,253
Cavalry of the Line	11,704	1,126	625	62	1,641	...	60	15,219
Royal Artillery	20,924	2,034	1,481	286	5,611	1	81	30,617
Royal Engineers	3,401	385	414	70	545	...	...	4,815
Foot Guards	4,544	685	251	28	482	...	2	5,992
Infantry of the Line	70,409	8,027	4,315	409	28,829	...	3,361	115,350
Colonial Corps	1,033	47	245	181	423	249	21	2,199
Commissariat and Transport Corps	1,975	149	192	84	357	...	...	2,757
Ordnance Staff Corps	348	41	99	20	75	...	...	583
Corps of Ordnance Artificers	19	3	11	...	...	...	...	33
Medical Staff Corps	1,601	120	123	71	275	...	...	2,190
General total	117,038	12,737	7,762	1,211	38,485	250	3,525	181,008
Proportion per 1000	662	72	43	6	217	...	...	1,000

EMIGRATION FROM THE UNITED KINGDOM, 1815-84.

Destination of Emigrants.

Period.	To United States.	To British North America.	To Australasia.	To all other Places.	Grand Totals.
1815-52	2,064,581	1,036,714	310,836	51,461	3,463,592
1853-60	983,625	159,807	397,389	41,654	1,582,475
1861-70	1,424,466	195,250	280,198	67,656	1,967,570
1871-80	1,531,851	232,213	313,106	151,226	2,228,396
1815-84	7,063,780	1,802,629	1,483,187	399,297	10,748,893

NOTE.—The total number of emigrants from Ireland only, to all places, between 1st May 1851 and 31st December 1884, was 2,989,327.

NATIONALITY OF EMIGRANTS IN 1853-84.

Period.	English.		Scotch.		Irish.		Total.
	No.	Percentage of Total.	No.	Percentage of Total.	No.	Percentage of Total.	
Three years, 1853-55.	211,013	30	62,514	9	421,672	61	695,199
Five years, 1856-60.	243,409	39	59,016	10	315,059	51	617,484
,, 1861-65.	236,838	33	62,461	9	418,497	58	717,796
,, 1866-70.	368,327	43	85,621	10	400,085	47	854,033
,, 1871-75.	545,015	56	95,055	10	329,467	34	969,537
Year 1876	73,396	67	10,097	9	25,976	24	109,469
,, 1877	63,711	67	8,653	9	22,831	24	95,195
,, 1878	72,323	64	11,087	10	29,492	26	112,902
,, 1879	104,275	64	18,703	11	41,296	25	164,274
,, 1880	111,845	49	22,056	10	93,641	41	227,542
,, 1881	139,976	58	26,826	11	76,200	31	243,002
,, 1882	162,992	58	32,242	12	84,132	30	279,366
,, 1883	183,236	57	31,139	10	105,743	33	320,118
,, 1884	147,660	61	21,953	9	72,566	30	242,179

IMMIGRANTS of British and Irish Origin that landed in the United Kingdom from Foreign Countries in each of the Years 1877 to 1884.

Country.	1877.	1878.	1879.	1880.	1881.	1882.	1883.	1884.
United States	44,878	34,040	20,048	26,518	29,781	28,468	46,703	61,466
British North America	5,687	6,204	3,497	4,688	5,761	6,097	7,021	8,861
Australasia	4,637	4,207	4,967	5,910	5,877	6,871	6,844	8,312
Other places	8,688	10,493	9,424	9,891	11,288	13,275	13,236	12,717
Total	63,890	54,944	37,936	47,007	52,707	54,711	73,804	91,356

REMITTANCES by Settlers in the United States and British North America to their Friends in the United Kingdom, in each year from 1848 to 1884.

Year.	Amount.	Year.	Amount.	Year.	Amount.
	£		£		£
1848	460,000	1861	374,061	1874	485,566
1849	540,000	1862	360,578	1875	354,356
1850	957,000	1863	383,286	1876	449,641
1851	990,000	1864	332,172	1877	667,564
1852	1,404,000	1865	481,580	1878	784,067
1853	1,439,000	1866	498,028	1879	855,631
1854	1,730,000	1867	543,029	1880	1,403,341
1855	873,000	1868	530,564	1881	1,505,794
1856	951,000	1869	639,335	1882	1,573,552
1857	593,165	1870	727,408	1883	1,611,206
1858	472,610	1871	702,488	1884	1,575,756
1859	520,019	1872	749,664		
1860	534,476	1873	724,040	Total	29,776,977*

* Settlers in Australasia remitted a further sum of £585,935 in the years 1875-84.

IRELAND.

SETTLERS IN UNITED STATES

who, at each of the last four Censuses, were Natives of the United Kingdom.

Census Years.	United Kingdom (total).	Natives of England.	Natives of Wales.	Natives of Scotland.	Natives of Ireland.	United Kingdom (country not specified).
1850	1,364,986	278,675	29,868	70,550	961,719	24,174
1860	2,224,743	431,692	45,763	108,518	1,611,304	27,466
1870	2,626,241	550,924	74,533	140,835	1,855,827	4,122
1880	2,772,169	662,676	83,302	170,136	1,854,571	1,484

THE IRISH GOVERNMENT.

I. *Expenses of Viceroyalty of Ireland.*

Salary of Lord Lieutenant of Ireland, chargeable on Consolidated Fund £20,000

Salaries of Household.

1 Private Secretary to the Lord Lieutenant, and clerks	£829
4 Aides-de-Camp, exclusive of military pay . . .	800
1 State Steward	506
1 Comptroller	414
1 Gentleman Usher	200
1 Chamberlain	200
1 Master of the Horse	200
3 Gentlemen in Waiting	443
1 Surgeon to the Household	100
1 State Porter	62
1 Sergeant of the Riding-house	30
1 Telegraphist at Viceregal Lodge . . .	91
Incidental expenses	85
Total expenses of household . .	£3,960

STATISTICAL TABLES. 185

Castle Chapel.

1 Chaplain, including house allowance	£335
1 Reading Clerk	42
1 Organist, including allowance for six boy choristers	240
2 Choristers	74
1 Keeper of the Chapel	98
Total for Chapel salaries	£789

Salaries and Allowances, Office of Arms, Queen's Plates, &c.

1 Ulster King at Arms, exclusive of £500 per annum as Keeper of State Papers	£920*
1 Athlone Pursuivant of Arms (in lieu of official fees)	20
1 Clerk in Office of Arms	30
1 Kettle Drummer's clothing	13
1 Porter and Messenger at Record Tower	74
1 Office Cleaner	30
Incidental expenses 1885-6 for Insignia and Banners of the Order of St. Patrick, emblazoning Arms, &c	70
QUEEN'S PLATES to be run for in Ireland	1,563
Total, Office of Arms, Queen's Plates, &c.	2,720
Pensions and Stationery	410
Total Expenditure 1885-86, exclusive of expenditure by Board of Public Works for maintenance of State residences, estimated at £10,091	£27,879

* The total fees and stamps received by the Crown in respect of Office of Arms in 1884-85 was £750.

THE IRISH GOVERNMENT—*Continued.*

II. *Expenses of Department of Chief Secretary to the Lord Lieutenant of Ireland.*

Salary of Chief Secretary	£4,425
Expenses of maintenance of residence, gardens, &c., at Phœnix Park	1,607
Salary of Under-Secretary	2,500
Expenses of maintenance of house in Dublin Castle	198
Expenses of maintenance of residence, demesne, &c., in Phœnix Park	1,000
Two Assistant Under-Secretaries	2,900
Two Principal Clerks	1,705
Nine First-class Clerks	3,406
One Draftsman of Bills	600
Allowances to Private Secretaries	620
Salaries of Junior Clerks, Messengers, &c.	3,647
Salaries of servants in London Office	3,108
Travelling and incidental expenses	1,990
Maintenance of offices by Board of Works	1,174
	£26,082

III. *Summary of Expenses of Irish Government.*

Expenses of Viceroyalty	£27,879
Maintenance of State Residences	10,091
Expenses of Department of Chief Secretary for Ireland	26,082
Total expenses of Irish Government	£64,052

AGRICULTURAL HOLDINGS IN IRELAND.

I. Area in Statute Acres under each Class in 1881.

Classification of Holdings, with the total Area under each Class.

Provinces.	Not exceeding 1 acre.	Above 1 and not exceeding 5 acres.	Above 5 and not exceeding 10 acres.	Above 10 and not exceeding 15 acres.	Above 15 and not exceeding 20 acres.	Above 20 and not exceeding 30 acres.	Above 30 and not exceeding 50 acres.	Above 50 and not exceeding 100 acres.	Above 100 and not exceeding 200 acres.	Above 200 and not exceeding 500 acres.	Above 500 acres.	Total.
	Acres.	Acres.	Acres.	Acres.	Acres.	Acres.	Acres.	Acres.	Acres.	Acres.	Acres.	Acres.
Leinster	4,748	52,376	100,669	118,205	144,544	272,575	522,422	863,769	868,098	866,760	571,856	4,386,022
Munster	3,050	31,874	74,463	100,588	150,470	348,516	776,752	1,425,538	1,187,734	922,808	536,924	5,558,717
Ulster	3,061	75,837	277,141	359,327	432,874	661,456	893,304	937,512	514,569	344,986	324,097	4,824,074
Connaught	2,562	51,883	212,087	267,631	296,956	371,101	390,613	370,191	367,245	435,911	754,083	3,520,263
Grand Total	13,421	211,970	664,360	845,751	1,024,844	1,653,648	2,583,091	3,597,010	2,937,646	2,570,465	2,186,870	18,289,076

AGRICULTURAL HOLDINGS IN IRELAND—Continued.

II. Number of Holdings rated separately in 1881.

PROVINCES.	£4 or under.	Over £4 and at or under £10.	Over £10 and at or under £15.	Holdings valued for rateable purposes at						Over £100.	Total Holdings.
				Over £15 and at or under £20.	Over £20 and at or under £30.	Over £30 and at or under £40.	Over £40 and at or under £50.	Over £50 and at or under £100.		
Leinster	38,825	32,251	15,695	10,229	12,036	6,806	4,288	8,738	5,926	134,794
Ulster	72,005	82,645	33,964	19,169	17,923	7,476	3,884	5,164	1,697	243,977
Munster	42,091	34,688	17,084	11,566	13,508	7,752	4,729	8,393	3,348	143,159
Connaught	65,228	47,350	10,969	4,577	3,862	1,669	1,075	2,129	1,396	138,255
Grand Total	218,199	196,934	77,712	45,541	47,329	23,703	13,976	24,424	12,367	660,185

AGRICULTURAL HOLDINGS IN IRELAND—Continued.

III. Number of Families Resident on each Class of Holdings in 1881.

Provinces.	Not exceeding 1 acre.	Above 1 and not exceeding 5 acres.	Above 5 and not exceeding 10 acres.	Above 10 and not exceeding 15 acres.	Above 15 and not exceeding 20 acres.	Above 20 and not exceeding 30 acres.	Above 30 and not exceeding 50 acres.	Above 50 and not exceeding 100 acres.	Above 100 and not exceeding 200 acres.	Above 200 and not exceeding 500 acres.	Above 500 acres.	Total Number of Families.
Leinster	5,978	15,550	12,059	9,207	8,686	11,966	16,237	17,924	12,866	9,848	5,356	125,677
Munster	4,321	9,728	9,735	8,237	9,441	16,330	25,425	31,897	19,608	11,059	4,657	150,438
Ulster	3,348	19,183	34,785	30,354	27,705	33,451	35,319	29,789	12,745	5,171	1,908	233,758
Connaught	3,301	14,211	26,797	21,850	17,741	16,172	11,575	6,786	4,086	3,069	3,298	128,886
Total Number	16,948	58,672	83,376	69,648	63,573	77,919	88,556	86,396	49,305	29,147	15,219	638,759

AGRICULTURAL HOLDINGS IN IRELAND—Continued.

IV. Number of each Class in 1881.

Classification of Holdings and Number in each Class.

Provinces.	Not exceeding 1 acre.	Above 1 and not exceeding 5 acres.	Above 5 and not exceeding 10 acres.	Above 10 and not exceeding 15 acres.	Above 15 and not exceeding 20 acres.	Above 20 and not exceeding 30 acres.	Above 30 and not exceeding 50 acres.	Above 50 and not exceeding 100 acres.	Above 100 and not exceeding 200 acres.	Above 200 and not exceeding 500 acres.	Above 500 acres.	Total number.
Leinster	6,091	16,470	12,849	9,269	8,152	10,851	13,184	12,417	6,381	3,007	715	99,386
Munster	3,976	9,985	9,268	7,724	8,248	13,651	19,519	20,289	8,745	3,240	690	105,335
Ulster	3,512	20,854	34,294	27,753	24,059	26,174	22,943	13,626	3,829	1,207	333	178,584
Connaught	3,300	14,442	25,988	20,678	16,554	14,828	10,063	5,234	2,615	1,427	675	115,804
Grand Total	16,879	61,751	82,399	65,424	57,013	65,504	65,709	51,566	21,570	8,881	2,413	499,109

OCCUPATIONS OF PERSONS

In the United Kingdom, according to Census of 1881.

CLASSES.	20 years and upwards.		All Ages.			Rate per cent.	
	Males.	Females.	Males.	Females.	Total.	Males.	Fem.
ENGLAND AND WALES:							
I. Professional	356,722	107,141	450,955	196,120	647,075	3·6	1·4
II. Domestic	215,621	1,332,504	258,508	1,545,302	1,803,810	2·4	11·6
III. Commercial	723,178	16,633	960,661	19,467	980,128	7·6	0·2
IV. Agricultural	1,054,195	47,248	1,318,344	64,840	1,383,184	10·4	0·5
V. Industrial	3,893,417	1,128,518	4,795,178	1,578,189	6,373,367	37·9	10·2
VI. Indefinite and Unproductive	670,429	853,985	4,856,256	9,930,619	14,786,875	38·1	76·1
Total	6,913,562	3,486,029	12,639,902	13,334,537	25,974,439	100·	100·
SCOTLAND:							
I. Professional	46,136	13,300	65,499	30,604	96,103	3·7	1·5
II. Domestic	21,549	101,546	25,292	151,273	176,565	1·4	7·7
III. Commercial	98,579	1,990	126,743	5,383	132,126	7·0	0·3
IV. Agricultural	172,377	38,432	215,215	54,322	269,537	11·9	2·7
V. Industrial	544,525	172,674	675,964	256,689	932,653	43·1	13·0
VI. Indefinite and Unproductive	34,680	745,909	690,762	1,437,827	2,128,589	32·9	74·8
Total	917,846	1,073,851	1,799,475	1,936,098	3,735,573	100·	100·
IRELAND:							
I. Professional	91,382	20,021	136,489	62,195	198,684	5·4	2·3
II. Domestic	26,072	313,364	34,068	392,093	426,161	1·3	14·8
III. Commercial	59,663	1,109	70,751	1,494	72,245	2·8	0·1
IV. Agricultural	757,112	84,656	902,010	95,946	997,956	35·6	3·6
V. Industrial	355,877	199,585	428,578	262,931	691,509	16·9	9·9
VI. Indefinite and Unproductive	47,410	845,639	961,381	1,826,900	2,788,281	38·0	69·3
Total	1,337,516	1,464,374	2,533,277	2,641,559	5,174,836	100·	100·
Total, United Kingdom	9,168,924	6,024,254	16,972,654	17,912,194	34,884,848	...	...

LANDOWNERS IN GREAT BRITAIN AND IRELAND.

Extracted from Doomsday Book of 1876.

CLASSIFICATION OF LANDS.	ENGLAND AND WALES.		SCOTLAND.		IRELAND.	
	Number of Owners.	Extent of Lands.	Number of Owners.	Extent of Lands.	No. of Owners.	Extent of Lands.
		Acres.		Acres.		Acres.
Total number of Owners of less than 1 acre	703,289	151,171	113,005	28,177	36,144	9,065
1 acre and under 10	121,983	478,679	9,471	29,327	6,892	28,968
10 ,, 50	72,640	1,750,080	3,469	77,619	7,746	195,525
50 ,, 100	25,839	1,791,606	1,213	86,483	3,479	250,147
100 ,, 500	32,317	6,827,347	2,367	556,372	7,989	1,955,536
500 ,, 1,000	4,799	3,317,678	826	582,741	2,716	1,915,528
1,000 ,, 2,000	2,719	3,799,307	591	835,242	1,803	2,514,743
2,000 ,, 5,000	1,815	5,529,190	587	1,843,378	1,198	3,675,267
5,000 ,, 10,000	581	3,974,725	250	1,726,869	452	3,154,628
10,000 ,, 20,000	223	3,098,675	159	2,150,111	185	2,478,493
20,000 ,, 50,000	66	1,917,076	103	3,071,728	90	2,558,850
50,000 ,, 100,000	3	194,939	44	3,025,616	14	1,023,677
100,000 acres and upwards	1	181,617	24	4,931,884	3	397,079
Areas not returned	6,448	...	11	...	...	...
Rentals not returned	113	1,424	11	1,147	...	...
Total	972,836	33,013,514	132,131	18,946,694	68,711	20,157,511

LANDS HELD IN IRELAND

By London City Livery Companies and the Irish Society, according to Doomsday Book, 1876.

Name of Company.	County in which Lands are situate.	Extent of Lands.	Government Valuation.
		Acreage.	£
Drapers' Company	Meath and Londonderry	27,588	15,415
Fishmongers' Company	Londonderry	20,509	9,159
Grocers' Company	ditto	11,638	6,457
Ironmongers' Company	ditto	12,714	8,032
Mercers' Company	ditto	21,241	11,740
Salters' Company	ditto	19,445	17,263
Skinners' Company	ditto	34,772	9,511
The Hon. the Irish Society	Donegal, Londonderry, and Tyrone	7,641	12,696
Total		155,548	90,273

NOTE.—It is believed that certain of the above lands have been sold to the tenants thereof, but no returns are available from which particulars of such sales could be given.

POLICE AND CONSTABULARY IN THE UNITED KINGDOM IN 1884.

	Number of Force.	Strength per 10,000 of Population.	Expense.		
			To Public Revenues.	Local Rates.	Total.
			£	£	
England and Wales.	34,999	13·5	1,353,145	2,122,855	3,476,000
Scotland	3,962	10·6	141,111	213,240	354,351
Ireland	14,523	28·0	1,402,752	167,545	1,570,297
United Kingdom Total.	53,484	15·3	2,897,008	2,503,640	5,400,648

CRIMINAL STATISTICS OF UNITED KINGDOM

For the Three Years 1882-84.

	Average Annual Number.			Percentage of Convictions.	Convictions per 10,000 of Population.	Convictions for Murder.		
	Committed for Trial.	Convicted.	Acquitted.			1882	1883	1884
England and Wales	14,775	11,060	3,338	74·9	4·2	22	23	38
Scotland	2,600	1,982	345	76·2	5·3	...	3	2
Ireland	3,417	1,847	1,401	53·7	3·6	21	11	5
Total, United Kingdom .	20,792	14,889	5,084	71·8	4·3	43	37	45 [1]

NOTE.—It will be seen from the foregoing table that during the three years 1882-84, Ireland had less crime, in proportion to its population, than either England or Scotland. If the number of convictions in Ireland had been increased to 75 per cent., the proportion of convictions per 10,000 of population would have been 4·9, or a less proportion than Scotland.

CRIMINAL STATISTICS OF IRELAND

For Years 1880–84.

Year.	Number committed for Trial.	Number Convicted.	Number Acquitted.	Offences specially reported by Constabulary.		
				Agrarian Outrages.	Other Offences.	Total.
1880	4,716	2,383	2,319	2,590	3,019	5,609
1881	5,311	2,698	2,443	4,439	3,349	7,788
1882	4,301	2,255	1,923	3,433	2,835	6,268
1883	3,025	1,740	919	870	1,665	2,535
1884	2,925	1,546	1,361	646	116	762

JUDICIAL RENTS IN IRELAND.

Result of Proceedings under "The Land Law (Ireland) Act, 1881," in fixing "Fair Rents" in 1881-84.

Year.	Number.	Fair Rents fixed.		Percentage of Reduction.	Year.
		Amount of Judicial Rents.	Amount of Former Rents.		
1881-82	43,726	£ 744,255	£ 925,728	19·6	1881-82
1883	71,971	1,046,735	1,282,848	18·4	1883
1884	41,743	561,631	674,050	16·7	1884
Total, 1881-84	157,440	2,352,621	2,882,626	18·4	1881-84

BOROUGH RATES IN IRELAND.

Eleven cities and towns are liable to the imposition of a Borough Rate—viz., Belfast, Clonmel, Cork, Drogheda, Dublin, Kilkenny, Limerick, Londonderry, Sligo, Waterford, and Wexford, of which the aggregate rateable valuation is about £1,800,000; and the average receipts and expenditure £750,000, and debt about £2,500,000.

TOWN RATES IN IRELAND.

There are 105 towns or local townships in Ireland having Commissioners to administer the same, pursuant to Acts of 9 Geo. IV. c. 82, and 17 & 18 Vic. c. 103, or special Acts, of which detailed particulars will be found in the Local Taxation (Ireland) Returns presented to Parliament. The average aggregate receipts and disbursements of town authorities, so constituted, is about £1,000,000, and debt about £400,000.

LOCAL TAXATION OF UNITED KINGDOM, 1880–83.

("From Statistical Abstracts of United Kingdom.")

	Year.	Local Taxes.	Government Subventions.	Loans.	Total Receipts, including Miscellaneous Receipts.	Total Expenditure.
England and Wales	1880-81	£ 31,837,141	£ 2,708,328	£ 12,937,528	£ 53,867,043	£ 53,397,306
	1881-82	32,932,454	2,865,584	15,006,778	57,475,679	56,545,392
	1882-83	35,368,065	3,323,827	10,649,567	53,784,312	53,420,923
Scotland	1880-81	3,890,000	546,000	905,000	6,047,000	6,067,451
	1881-82	4,164,741	593,103	1,063,396	6,314,172	6,051,574
	1882-83	4,130,296	586,020	901,191	6,198,684	5,952,171
Ireland	1880-81	3,111,802	114,857	401,504	3,872,249	3,937,833
	1881-82	3,140,460	115,941	396,249	3,915,228	4,068,533
	1882-83	3,276,577	114,813	402,891	4,088,925	4,156,387
Total, United Kingdom	1880-81	38,838,943	3,369,185	14,244,032	63,786,292	63,402,590
	1881-82	40,237,655	3,574,628	16,466,423	67,705,079	66,665,499
	1882-83	42,771,938	4,024,660	11,953,649	64,071,921	63,529,481

GROSS IMPERIAL REVENUE OF UNITED KINGDOM

From Customs and Inland Revenue, for the Three Financial Years ended 25th March 1885.

	Year.	Customs.	Inland Revenue.			Total Customs and Inland Revenue.
			Excise.	Stamps.	Taxes.	
England and Wales	1883	£16,167,991	£18,137,739	£10,155,627	£13,307,541	£57,768,898
	1884	16,155,958	18,196,819	10,073,430	12,180,470	56,606,677
	1885	16,902,396	17,757,577	10,345,460	13,180,644	58,186,077
Scotland	1883	1,679,366	5,093,958	1,082,935	1,378,327	9,234,586
	1884	1,700,281	5,145,446	1,122,662	1,135,580	9,103,969
	1885	1,782,619	5,027,093	1,018,457	1,329,734	9,157,903
Ireland	1883	1,986,954	4,585,160	629,597	556,490	7,758,201
	1884	1,958,319	4,555,485	650,495	581,041	7,745,340
	1885	2,038,302	4,521,106	655,922	601,952	7,817,282
Total, United Kingdom	1883	19,834,311	27,816,857	11,868,159	15,265,975	74,785,302
	1884	19,814,558	27,897,750	11,846,587	13,897,091	73,455,986
	1885	20,723,317	27,305,776	12,019,839	15,112,330	75,161,262

NOTE.—The revenue from Post Office, Telegraphs, and other miscellaneous services for the United Kingdom amounts to about £15,000,000.

STATISTICAL TABLES.

IMPERIAL EXPENDITURE FOR IRELAND.

PROVIDED FOR IN CIVIL SERVICE ESTIMATES AND CONSOLIDATED FUND IN 1885–6.

I. *Items included in Civil Service Estimates*, 1885–6.

CLASS I.—*Public Works and Buildings.*

Rates on Government Property	£32,145
Public Buildings	221,784
Royal University Buildings	27,428
Science and Art Buildings (Dublin)	31,000
Total, Class I.	312,357

CLASS II.—*Salaries and Expenses of Public Departments.*

Lord Lieutenant's Household	£7,469
Chief Secretary's Office	43,382
Charitable Donations and Bequests Office	2,152
Local Government Board	139,628
Public Works Office	56,111
Record Office	6,756
Registrar-General's Office	16,126
Valuation and Boundary Survey	23,804
Total, Class II.	295,428

CLASS III.—*Law and Justice.*

Law Charges and Criminal Prosecutions	£79,206
Supreme Court of Judicature	91,222
Court of Bankruptcy	10,300
Admiralty Court Registry	1,285
Registry of Deeds	17,510
Registry of Judgments	2,338
Land Commission	78,677
County Court Officers, &c.	96,316
Dublin Metropolitan Police (including Police Courts)	145,817
Constabulary	1,380,091
Prisons, Ireland	158,441
Reformatory and Industrial Schools	101,150
Dundrum Criminal Lunatic Asylum	6,847
Total, Class III.	2,169,200

IRELAND.

IMPERIAL EXPENDITURE FOR IRELAND.—*Continued.*

CLASS IV.—*Education, Science and Art.*

Public Education	£786,303
Teachers' Pension Office	2,013
Endowed Schools Commissioners . . .	670
National Gallery	2,501
Queen's Colleges	12,628
Royal Irish Academy	2,000

Total, Class IV. .   806,115

CLASS VI.—*Superannuations and Charities.*

Pauper Lunatics	98,200
Hospitals and Infirmaries	16,747
Miscellaneous Charitable and other Allowances.	2,971

Total, Class VI. .   117,918

Total provided for in Civil Service Estimates   £3,701,018

II. *Items chargeable to Consolidated Fund,* 1884–5.

Salary of Lord Lieutenant	£20,000
Salaries of Judges of Superior and County Courts .	115,554
Pensions for Judicial Services	21,079
Pensions of Officials of Courts of Justice . .	2,735
Grant to Queen's Colleges	21,470
King's Inn Library, Dublin, under Copyright Act	433
Allowances, under 41 George III. c. 32, to Lord Mayor and Citizens of Dublin	715
Under-Librarian at Marsh's Library, Dublin .	26
Rent of Ground near Carrickfergus Castle . .	14

Total paid, 1884–5 out of Consolidated Fund   182,026

Grand total of Imperial Expenditure for Ireland, exclusive of proportion of Army and Navy expenses. . .   £3,883,044

LOANS FOR PUBLIC WORKS, &c., IN IRELAND.

I. *Loans made by Commissioners of Public Works in Ireland, under the provisions of the Act 1 and 2 Wm. IV. cap. 33, and subsequent Acts.*

Objects.	Total issued to 31st March 1885.		
	£	s.	d.
I. PUBLIC WORKS LOAN FUND :—			
For Roads, Court-houses, &c.	737,569	7	1
To Local Boards for Improvement of Townships	123,550	0	0
Roads, Bridges, &c.	200,477	0	4
Inland Navigation Works Improvement	69,950	0	0
Public Buildings, Erection and Completion	52,100	0	0
Railways, in aid of Construction	963,239	5	8
In aid of Quarries, Mines, &c.	15,283	0	0
Sundry Harbours, Docks, &c , Construction	431,058	6	1
Fishery Piers and Harbours	53,279	6	6
Reclamation of Waste Lands	96,000	0	0
Labourers' Dwellings in Towns	167,592	15	2
Artisans' Dwellings	81,000	0	0
Glebe Loans	354,947	0	0
Public Health	1,088,204	1	1
River Drainage, and Navigation	2,082,052	7	3
River Drainage Maintenance	39,313	10	11
River Drainage	581,390	18	10
Public Works Loans	491,444	19	8
Repairs of Roads, Bridges	133,640	16	1
Land Improvement, Preliminary Expenses	58,500	0	0
Repairs of Fishery Piers	14,232	9	2
Maintenance of Navigation Works	2,430	0	0
Gaols and Bridewells	892,758	6	9
Lunatic Asylums Buildings	1,332,378	7	3
Building Schools	10,293	5	7
Relief of Distress	15,756	0	0
Seed Supply	647,562	11	10
Emigration	11,675	3	10
Improvement of Lands, 10 Vic. c. 32 :—For Drainage, Farm Buildings, Labourers' Dwellings, Planting for Shelter, Scutch-mills, &c.	3,737,656	1	5

(*Continued next page.*)

IRELAND.

LOANS FOR PUBLIC WORKS, &c.—*Continued.*

	£	s.	d.
National School Teachers' Residences	44,879	0	0
Dispensary Houses	26,928	0	0
Land Law Act, 44 & 45 Vic. c. 49, s. 31 :—			
Advances to Tenants for Improvements	371,271	0	0

II. LAND ACT FUND, 33 and 34 Vic. c. 46 :—
Advances to Tenants for purchase of their holdings,
authorized 1870–81 . . . . . . 518,416 13 0

III. IRISH CHURCH FUND ACT, 43 Vic. c. 4, and
43 and 44 Vic. c. 14 :—

Improvement of Lands	918,245	17	9
Public Health	38,535	10	0
Baronial Works	271,083	0	10
Relief of Distress	11,383	13	4
Ditto, Grants	19,069	3	0
Arterial Drainage	6,136	1	0

(£1,264,453 5s 11d)

Grand total of Loans by Irish Board of Works £16,711,282 19 5

The balance of principal and interest outstanding on 31st March 1885 was £7,531,956.

II. *Loans made in Ireland by the Public Works Loan Commissioners, London, under various Acts.*

OBJECTS.	Total Loans to March 31, 1885.	Balance, Principal and Interest outstanding March 31, 1885.
	£	£
Harbours	40,850	2,900
Belfast and Co. Down Railway	164,804	72,915
Railways	2,686,750	415,995
Do., Temporary Advances	159,356	34,521
Burial Boards	18,678	967
Waterworks	479,000	308,095
Sewage Utilization	11,035	1,849
Workhouses	2,000	200
Total	3,562,473	837,442

III. LOANS made by the Irish Land Commission, showing the amount advanced by way of Loan under "The Land Law (Ireland) Act, 1881," and "The Tramways and Public Companies (Ireland) Act, 1883."

Objects.	Total issued to March 31, 1885.	Balances Outstanding.		
		Principal.		Interest.
		In Arrear.	Not Due.	
	£ s. d.	£ s. d.	£ s. d.	£ s. d.
LAND LAW (IRELAND) ACT, 1881:				
For purchases by tenants from their landlords (24th and 35th sections)	181,498 0 0	159 8 7	178,518 9 3	149 12 11
For purchases by tenants from the Land Commission (26th section)	48,933 0 0	2 9 8	47,379 9 10	5 19 4
For purchases by persons not being the occupying tenants (27th section)	245 0 0	1 13 2	242 15 10	3 19 4
In payment of arrears of rent due by tenants (59th section)	18,793 10 11	36 1 5	1,542 0 11	19 1 4
TRAMWAYS AND PUBLIC COMPANIES (IRELAND) ACT, 1883:				
For purchase of estates by public companies (13th section)	42,300 0 0	......	42,300 0 0	......
	291,769 10 11	199 12 10	269,982 15 10	178 12 11

SUMMARY OF IRISH LOANS.

I. By Commissioners of Public Works, Ireland . £16,711,283
II. By Public Works Loan Commissioners, London . 3,562,473
III. By Irish Land Commission 291,769

Grand Total £20,565,525

VALUE OF EXPORTS AND IMPORTS OF THE UNITED KINGDOM

In the Three Years ended 31st December 1884.

Ports.	1882.	1883.	1884.
England and Wales ...	£ 219,569,672	£ 217,950,777	£ 211,802,613
Scotland	20,876,705	20,952,830	20,450,785
Ireland	1,029,785	895,866	771,844
Total Exports ...	241,467,162	239,799,473	233,025,242
Total Imports ...	413,019,608	426,891,579	390,018,569

EXPORTS FROM IRELAND OF CATTLE, SHEEP, AND SWINE.

Imported from Ireland into Great Britain, as compared with Imports from Foreign Countries.

Based on "Annual Statement of the Trade of the United Kingdom," and Privy Council Returns.

	Year.	Oxen, Bulls, and Cows.	Calves.	Sheep and Lambs.	Swine.
		Number.	Number.	Number.	Number.
Numbers from Ireland ...	1882	722,581	59,693	558,404	502,906
	1883	509,940	46,927	460,729	461,017
	1884	644,598	71,245	533,285	456,678
Numbers from Foreign Countries	1882	309,359	34,340	1,124,391	15,670
	1883	427,694	47,056	1,116,115	38,863
	1884	371,010	54,497	945,042	26,437
		£	£	£	£
Value—Irish Imports	1882	15,354,846	280,059	1,270,369	1,846,083
	1883	10,868,009	218,993	1,036,640	1,613,560
	1884	13,915,247	336,632	1,213,223	2,294,807
Value — Foreign Imports ...	1882	6,573,878	161,112	2,557,990	57,521
	1883	9,112,723	219,519	2,518,382	133,130
	1884	8,013,426	257,594	2,149,704	84,153

AVERAGE VALUE PER HEAD OF LIVE CATTLE, SHEEP, AND PIGS,

Imported into the United Kingdom from Foreign Countries and British Possessions, in each of undermentioned years.

Years.	Cattle. Oxen and Bulls.	Cattle. Cows.	Cattle. Calves.	Sheep. (including Lambs.)	Pigs.
	£ s. d.	£ s. d.	£ s. d.	£ s. d.	£ s. d.
1865	18 14 1	16 5 1	4 6 7	1 19 1	2 14 0
1870	17 19 11	15 14 1	4 4 4	1 14 4	3 14 6
1875	21 10 3	18 15 11	4 15 3	2 4 4	3 10 8
1880	22 0 11	18 5 7	4 14 11	2 8 1	3 9 10
1884	21 19 10	19 12 0	4 14 6	2 5 5	3 3 7

CORN STATISTICS.

Average Prices of Wheat, Barley, and Oats, per imp. qr. in England and Wales, in the undermentioned years.

Year.	Wheat.	Barley.	Oats.
	s. d.	s. d.	s. d.
1801	119 6	68 6	37 0
1811	95 3	42 3	27 7
1821	56 1	26 0	29 6
1831	66 4	38 0	25 4
1841	64 4	32 10	22 5
1851	38 6	24 9	18 7
1861	55 4	36 1	23 9
1871	56 8	36 2	25 2
1881	45 4	31 11	21 9
1884	35 9	30 8	20 3

NOTE.—The average price of wheat alone per imperial quarter in 1756 was 40·1s.; in 1761, 26·8s.; in 1771, 48·6s.; in 1781, 46s.; and in 1791, 48·6s.

COMPARATIVE AGRICULTURAL VALUES

In England at different periods, as estimated by Sir James Caird.

	1770.	1850.	1880.
Rent of land per acre.	13s.	27s.	30s.
Price of bread per lb.	1½d.	1¼d.	1½d.
,, meat ,,	3¾	5d.	9d.
,, butter ,,	6d.	1s.	1s. 8d.
Wages, agricultural labourers, per week	7s. 3d.	9s. 7d.	14s.
Rent of labourer's cottage, per week	8d.	1s. 5d.	2s.

VALUATION OF PROPERTY

By Rating Authorities in England, Scotland, and Ireland, at undermentioned periods.

	Year 1877.	Year 1881.	Year 1885.
	£	£	£
England and Wales, estimated rental	146,995,016	165,143,300	169,835,285
Scotland, valuation	21,846,839	22,689,000	23,559,870
Ireland, valuation	13,619,516	13,766,600	13,883,972

AGRICULTURAL PRODUCE IN IRELAND.

Prices at undermentioned periods, according to Acts of Parliament, &c.

Produce.	Prices per cwt. of 112 lbs.		
	Acts of 1826, 1836, and 1846.	Act of 1852.	Proposed Act of 1877.
	s. d.	s. d.	s. d.
Wheat	10 0	7 6	10 0
Oats	6 0	4 10	7 8
Barley	7 6	5 6	8 4
Butter	69 0	65 4	121 4
Beef	33 0	35 6	70 0
Mutton	34 6	41 0	74 8
Pork	25 6	32 0	51 4
Flax	......	49 0	60 0

NOTE.—The prices in Act of 1852 were the basis of the valuation known as "Griffith's Valuation."

AVERAGE PRICES OF LIVE STOCK IN IRELAND

At undermentioned periods.

Description of Stock.	Prices. Census Estimate, 1841.	Prices. Royal Dublin Society's Estimate, 1876.
	£ s. d.	
Horses	8 0 0	£22
Horned cattle	6 10 0	£5 to £18
Sheep	1 2 0	30s. to 50s.
Pigs	1 5 0	50s. to £5

IRISH CHURCH SURPLUS.

[32 and 33 Vict. cap. 42.]

Estimated value of Property of Disestablished Church of Ireland, about	£17,500,000
Compensations paid for Clerical and other interests in connection with Disestablished Church, and estimated value of outstanding interests, about	£10,500,000
Approximate surplus	£7,000,000

The surplus has been appropriated in the following manner, mainly in relief of payments out of Imperial Exchequer :—

Compensation to Royal College of St. Patrick's, Maynooth, being 14 years' purchase of grant paid up to 1870, out of Consolidated Fund of United Kingdom*	£372,331
Compensation to Presbyterian and other Nonconforming Bodies in Ireland for loss, in 1870, of grant by Parliament of "The Regium Donum," first granted in 1672 by Charles the Second, amounting to about £38,000 per annum*	750,000
Intermediate Education Grant of 1878, producing £32,500 per annum	1,000,000
Pension Fund for National School Teachers, granted 1879, producing £39,000 per annum	1,300,000
Grants sanctioned under Relief of Distress Acts, 1880, repayable by terminable annuities, of which amount required is believed to be under £1,300,000†	1,500,000
Grant of £20,000 per annum in 1881, as an endowment for Royal University of Ireland, capital value, about‡	600,000
Grants under Arrears of Rent (Ireland) Act, 1882, about	950,000
Sea Fisheries grants	250,000
Grants to distressed Unions, say	10,500
Total grants	£6,732,831
Estimated net unappropriated surplus, exclusive of sums repayable in respect of loans under Relief of Distress Acts, &c.	£267,169

---

* The aggregate saving to the Imperial Exchequer during the fifteen years 1870–85, by the abolition of the "Maynooth" and "Regium Donum" grants, has been estimated at about one million sterling.

† It has been estimated that, owing to the special terms as to interest on these grants, there will be an ultimate loss of about £500,000 to the surplus by Relief of Distress Acts.

‡ The parliamentary grant for the Queen's University in Ireland, superseded by the Royal University in 1882, was about £5,000 per annum.

PARLIAMENTARY AND ELECTORAL STATISTICS.

I. REGISTERED ELECTORS, AND PERCENTAGE OF ELECTORS POLLED, &c., 1885.

TABLE showing Population according to Census of 1881, estimated number of Registered Electors, and Electors polled at General Election of 1885, and percentage of Electors who polled for Liberal, Conservative and Nationalist Candidates respectively.

Constituencies.	Population, 1881.	Registered Electors, 1885.	Electors polled, 1885.*	Percentage of Registered Electors polled.	Percentage of Electors polled for		
					Liberals.	Conservatives.	Nationalists.
		Number.	Number.				
England and Wales	25,974,439	4,397,000	3,513,300	80·6	52·4	47·4	0·2
Scotland	3,735,573	573,000	438,100	76·5	64·9	35·1	...
Ireland	5,174,836	742,000	439,300	59·1	6·9	25·4	67·7
Total, U.K.	34,884,848	5,712,000	4,390,700	76·9	49·1	44·1	6·8

* Exclusive of uncontested elections.

PARLIAMENTARY AND ELECTORAL STATISTICS.

II. CONSTITUTION OF HOUSE OF COMMONS ELECTED NOVEMBER AND DECEMBER 1885.

TABLE *showing number and percentage of Liberals, Conservatives and Nationalists returned as Members of Parliament, and the proportion of Members to aggregate Population—Electors and Voters.*

Constituencies.	Party Returns.				Percentage of Members of each Party.			Proportion of Members to		
	L.	C.	N.	Total.	L.	C.	N.	Population.	Electors.	Voters.*
England and Wales	271	223	1	495	54.8	45.0	0.2	1 for 52,473	1 for 8,883	1 for 7,097
Scotland	62	10	...	72	86.1	13.9	...	1 for 51,883	1 for 7,951	1 for 6,084
Ireland	...	18	85	103	...	17.5	82.5	1 for 50,241	1 for 7,203	1 for 4,265
United Kingdom	333	251	86	670	49.7	37.5	12.8	1 for 52,067	1 for 8,525	1 for 6,553

* Uncontested elections are not taken into account in calculation of proportion of members to voters.

NOTE.—The largest population represented by one Member is that of "St. George's," Hanover Square, London, 89,537; and the smallest population (Pontefract), 15,332. Twelve constituencies have a population of over 80,000 each, and eighteen constituencies have a population of under 20,000 each.

ESTIMATED NUMBER OF ELECTORS OF UNCONTESTED CONSTITUENCIES.

Parties.	Electors, England and Wales.	Electors, Scotland.	Electors, Ireland.	Members returned unopposed.
Liberals	63,000	30,300	...	14
Conservatives	23,800	6,400	23,500	10
Nationalists	...	...	133,400	20
Total	86,800	36,700	156,900	44

AVERAGE PRICES REALIZED FROM SALES OF IRISH ESTATES,

With Parliamentary Title, in Land Judges' Courts, Dublin.

1865–68	1869–74	1875–77	1878–80	1881–83	1884
Years' purchase.	Years' purchase.	Years' purchase.	Years' purchase.	Years' purchase.	Years' purchase
21¼	21⅛	20⅜	17·7	15·8	19·8

NOTE.—The highest average of 23¼ years' purchase on net rentals was attained in the year 1871; and the lowest, 14·9 years' purchase, in 1883.

www.ingramcontent.com/pod-product-compliance
Lightning Source LLC
Chambersburg PA
CBHW021842230426
43669CB00008B/1054